Baltimore's Two Cross Keys Villages

Baltimore's Two Cross Keys Villages

✦

One Black. One White.

...and the leaders who created the world around them

Jim Holechek

iUniverse, Inc.
New York Lincoln Shanghai

Baltimore's Two Cross Keys Villages
One Black. One White.

iUniverse, Inc.

For information address:
iUniverse, Inc.
2021 Pine Lake Road, Suite 100
Lincoln, NE 68512
www.iuniverse.com

COVER: The inset photograph shows a few of the remaining homes in the original African American Cross Keys Village. The background photograph is of Palmer Green, one of the hamlets in The Village of Cross Keys built by The Rouse Company. Both villages are located on Falls Road in northern Baltimore City. Cover designed by the author.

Manuscript and graphics were prepared for iUniverse format by CLS Business Services at cheryl@initialweb.com

ISBN: 0-595-27358-0

Printed in the United States of America

Dedicated to Edwin "Ned" A. Daniels, 1925–2002.

Contents

Introduction xi

CHAPTER 1   Cross Keys Village, The Road and Falls 1

CHAPTER 2   Vital Family Community 15

CHAPTER 3   Villagers Remember 28

CHAPTER 4   Upcountry, the Chapel and Marie 45

CHAPTER 5   The Island Village 75

CHAPTER 6   The Modern Urban Community is Born 88

CHAPTER 7   The Tough Work Begins 109

CHAPTER 8   DeVito Saves the Company 126

CHAPTER 9   The Flawed House 145

CHAPTER 10   The Villages and Their Futures 153

APPENDIX 155

   •   *Buildings and Management of The Village of Cross Keys* *159*
   •   *Cross Keys Shops, Past and Present* *161*
   •   *General Map* *163*
   •   *Scott Settlement Historic District Map* *164*

Bibliography 167

   •   *Baltimore County Map* *171*

Index 173

Acknowledgment

When I discovered that developer Jim Rouse may have named The Village of Cross Keys after an adjacent African American community my curiosity was stirred.

Betty and Will Standiford of Roland Park helped get me started on the local history that impacted on this book. Then Ann Walsh introduced me to the dynamic Holly Parker and her husband, Tony, a direct descendant of Tobias, the slave who saved his master's life and was freed.

Back and forth I went, discovering along the way the rich histories of these villages of the Jones Falls Valley and Falls Road. Anna Marie Julius Scott Brown at 92 is an icon of the area. She too is a direct descendant of Tobias and is the thread between the Historic Black Scott Settlement in Bare Hills and the black Cross Keys Village, both on The Falls Road.

Special thanks to Matt DeVito, the former CEO, president and chairman of The Rouse Company, the senior officer who explained the workings of his good friend, Jim Rouse. But it was Ned Daniels who had been one of the project managers during the construction of The Village of Cross Keys whose story-telling abilities created the excitement for the more contemporary chapters of the book.

There has been much published about The Rouse Company, but little written about The Village of Cross Keys, the residential community built on the former golf course, once owned by the Baltimore Country Club and before that by Robert Goodloe Harper, the illustrious lawyer, army general, and U. S. Representative and Senator from two states. He also was the son-in-law of the last surviving signer of the Declaration of Independence, Charles Carroll of Carrollton.

So while the research road was long, its turns and forks led to many interesting and helpful places and people. My thanks first go to the professionals like Jeff Korman at the Maryland Room of the Central Enoch Pratt Library, Barbara Kellner of the Columbia Archives, Frances O'Neill, Ed Arthur, Mary Markey and others of the Maryland Historical Society, as well as Tom Hollowak of the library at the University of Baltimore and Kathy Harig of Roland Park Library.

Special recognition to Gail O'Donovan who spearheaded the effort to save the historic "colored" St. John's Chapel, parsonage and cemetery in Ruxton. Her foresight and notes were so helpful in finally recording this important corner of African American history.

It was all of the people who recognized the part they played in local history that was truly exciting. So my deepest thanks go to Amy Davis, Cary Beehler, Bill Temmink, Carol Runion, Jack Gillett, Marge Osborne, Carolyn Scott LeVere, Monk Askew, Betty Cooke, Bill Steinmetz, Ruth Shaw, Roy Waldorf, George Shapiro, Mike Grier, Joan Reed, Valerie Whiting, Delores Silva, Frank Rybczn-ski, Barry Grube, Ray Wheeler, Michael Douglass, Delores Johnson, Joe Coale, Randall Beirne, Fred Hinze, Sarah Lord, Sandia Ross, Jim Burns, Al Kilberg, Ralph Clayton, Sally Willse, Aileen Gabby, Bill Boykin, Brian Ivins, Dan Toomey, Paul Lockwood, Gilbert Sandler, Inez Glorioso, Dennis Dickerson, Charlie Tipper, Janet Reynolds, Tom Spies, Scott Ditch, Richard Altman, Jim and Thelma Lightner, W. Boulton Kelly, Jim Waesche, Herb Harwood, Marie Scott Brown, and William Hollifield.

Also, Tom Bruggman, Josh Olsen, Margaret Doyle, David Widows, Patty Rouse, David Drake, Bob Erlandson, Marie Fischer Cooke, Richard Parsons, Rupel Marshall, Lewis V. Baldwin, Frank DeFilippo, Frank Goodlake, Libby Rouse, Polly Shannahan, Adam Blumenthal, Eric Papenfuse, Wiley Baxter, Michelle Schiffer, Florence Sokol, Jesse Hawkins, Sally Kutch, Ernestine Palmer, Ben Mason, June Hawkins, Jerry Hynson, Ed Chaney, Garland Crosby, Sharon McBride, Tony Lee, Bernard McBride, John McBride, Charles Seabreeze, Geral-dine Epps, Reita Bryant, Ann Carter, Robin Munson, Walter Gordon, David Tripp and Ruth Hill.

Thanks, too, to an old friend who cast a cold eye on the manuscript, Tom Mallonee. To Scott Ditch, an acquaintance from the past who has become a real friend, thanks for the input. Scott was a vice president with Rouse and made sure the forty years of The Village of Cross Keys story were accurate and chronologi-cally correct. He, John W. McGrain, Baltimore County Historian, and Sarah Lord all gave gracious encouragement at the right times. And without the help of a special woman, Vertelle Hall, there never would have been the reunion of former residents of Cross Keys Village. She led me to Paul Johnson, a brilliant teacher who remembered, not only the people of the African American Cross Keys Village, but many of the anecdotes that made the stories come alive.

Finally, in the eighteen months it took to produce this work, I want to thank my wife, Pat, for all her help in spelling, chauffeuring to the libraries and patience with my being closeted alone so long with my computer.

Introduction

This story of the historic Jones Falls Valley begins with the tale of two communities: Cross Keys Village, a 200-year-old largely African American enclave, *and* The Village of Cross Keys, precursor of the new town of Columbia, Maryland. The two Cross Keys villages are set nearly adjacent to one another on Falls Road just west of exclusive Roland Park in Baltimore. It is also about two leaders of the land: Robert Goodloe Harper and James Wilson Rouse. There are other men and women, of course, who helped make their villages, up and down the fast flowing Jones Falls, an important part of Greater Baltimore.

Robert Goodloe Harper was born ten years before the American Revolution in Fredricksburg, Virginia. As a teenager he joined a militia cavalry unit and helped push Cornwallis out of Yorktown. His family wasn't wealthy but managed to send their only son to Princeton where he tutored younger students, was recognized for his scholarly achievements and moved into prominent social circles.

After graduation, Robert went to Charleston, South Carolina, and with the help of college contacts, received the attention of notables who carefully guided him through law studies and, finally, the bar. His oratory and persuasion led him to a career in state politics, and later as a Federalist to the U. S. House from North Carolina. Then he came to Maryland where he had been encouraged to settle and open a law practice. Here, he also became active in state politics and was elected a U. S. Senator.

Having met Charles Carroll of Carrollton on his jaunts to Congress in Philadelphia, the dashing Harper recognized the power and wisdom of the wealthiest man in the colonies. Whether that attracted him to court and marry Carroll's youngest daughter, Catherine, it's hard to say. Kitty, as she was known, was raised at Doughoregan Manor in Howard County and educated in England. Several years after their marriage in 1801, Charles Carroll initially purchased land in Baltimore County (now in Baltimore City) from Nicholas Hooper and gave it to Kitty for a summer home. It would be known as Oakland (now part of Roland Park). Part of the initial 267.68 acres has been traced to Charles Merryman, who was granted his lands by Cecil Calvert, the second Lord Baltimore, once he took control of his province in 1634. Later the property was bought by Colonel Charles Ridgely, then it went to Nicholas Hooper, finally passing to the Harpers.

The Harper estate grew through 1818, and contained an irregular rectangle of four hundred and forty acres—from Roland Avenue west to Jones Falls and Coldspring Lane north to Northern Parkway—much of it was premier land overlooking the narrowing Jones Falls Valley. It included tumbling brooks and at least a dozen pure water springs. Tucked along its southern boundary were several free-black enclaves. In 1898, the Oakland property was sold by Harper heirs to the Roland Park Company to form part of Baltimore's exclusive community.

Robert Goodloe Harper, the distinguished South Carolina and Maryland statesman, was son-in-law of Charles Carroll of Carrollton, the longest living signer of The Declaration of Independence. Carroll gave Oakland (now part of Roland Park) to his daughter Catherine as a belated wedding gift in 1804. Harper operated it as a wheat farm (now The Village of Cross Keys) with nine slaves.——Maryland Historic Society.

In a flat meadow in Roland Park several hundred yards up Englewood Road from Falls Road was the Harper farmyard, which in 1810 was comprised of an overseer's house, at least two slave quarters, barn, stable, smokehouse, ice house and a unique two-story springhouse dairy among those designed by Benjamin H. Latrobe, a close friend of Robert Harper. In 1931, the brick, fieldstone and stucco classic Greek dairy was disassembled and rebuilt in the west gardens of the Baltimore Museum of Art where it stands today. The Oakland smokehouse was never moved from its original location, but incorporated at an angle within the Wiley M. Baxter house that was built around it in 1926. Elizabeth Baxter, whose idea it was to retain the old smokehouse, is to be commended for her interest in historic preservation. The fireplace, roof and chimney had been removed according to Fred Hinze, the Edgevale Road home's present owner. The stuccoed smokehouse-garage measures 22 feet square with windows 49 inches by 38 inches and wall thickness of 27 inches.

Had the Oakland farm buildings survived, they would have overlooked the Springhouse Condominium Apartments at 5203 Falls Road, converted from the 1897 brick car barn and repair shop for the No. 25 trolley of the Baltimore & Northern Railway. The car barn was closed about 1936 and sold in 1946 when it was first renovated into the Robert E. Lee Apartments. During the rebuilding process, work pits were filled with old parts of trolley cars and tracks. In 2001, one of the apartment owners said some of her kitchen floor had collapsed revealing parts of the old streetcars.

Above: Present owner Fred Hinze stands by the original smoke house portion of the garage. The stucco building was ingeniously incorporated into the house when it was built in 1926. It is located on Edgevale Road, the former property of Robert Goodloe Harper's Oakland estate in Roland Park. It was a preservation idea of Elizabeth Baxter when she and her husband built the home.
Below: The Oakland springhouse designed by Benjamin H. Latrobe, overseer's house on left and slave quarters on right. Photograph was taken just before the springhouse was disassembled and rebuilt on the west grounds of the Baltimore Museum of Arts in 1931. The house in the far right background is at 401 Edgevale Road (northeast corner of Edgevale and Deepdene).

The friend of many, Robert Goodloe Harper was promoted to major general at the Battle of North Point (Maryland) in 1814. Toward the end of his life, he became active in the colonization movement to send free and slave African Americans back to Africa. In *An Eyewitness History of Slavery in America*, it reports "Altogether the [American Colonization] Society managed to send off only some 11,000 [freeborn and slave] emigrants over more than 40 years." In *Maryland: A Middle Temperament 1634–1980*, it states: "By late summer of 1834, Maryland in Liberia, as settlers called Cape Palmas, had grown into a village of twelve private houses, a fort, jail, community kitchen, church, school, and several buildings for the shelter of new arrivals."

When he died of a massive heart attack in 1825, Harper was virtually broke. Due to intemperate speculation in real estate, any of its remaining value was owed to Charles Carroll who several times had rescued him from bankruptcy. His funeral drew a parade of soldiers, lawyers and grieving family members that proceeded from Baltimore City to the hillside family cemetery at Oakland.

Harper's granddaughter, Emily Harper Pennington, later had his remains and four others of the family re-interred in Baltimore's Greenmount Cemetery. Apparently the five Oakland family bodies were first buried in the Pennington lots 31 & 33 in section M, then moved after Emily Harper Pennington bought the corner lot 121 in area U, sometime after December 18, 1882. The old Oakland cemetery had been located at the far northern edge of the property near St. Mary's Seminary.

Urban developer and social engineer James Wilson Rouse was the other notable gentleman in our story. A contemporary of the twentieth century, he was born on April 26, 1914, in Brooklets, a frame manor house once located at the site of 219 Hanson Street in Easton, Maryland. It had been the home of its builder, Dr. John C. Earle, until the summer of 1909 when the Rouses occupied the estate.

Robert Goodloe Harper died in 1825, and his body was buried in the family cemetery in Oakland. When the land was sold to the Roland Park Company, Harper's and other bodies were moved to Greenmount Cemetery by his granddaughter, Emily Harper Pennington. At right is Harper's gravestone designed by architect and lawyer John H. B. Latrobe, son of architect Benjamin Latrobe. The monument in the center is for Harriet L. Harper, granddaughter, and Catherine Carroll Harper, wife, and the one on the left is for son Charles Carroll Harper and his wife, Charlotte Chiffelle Harper.

Willard G. Rouse, Jim's father, was a lawyer and hopeful politician. Together with his mother, Lydia, they had moved from Belair, Maryland, to the Eastern Shore tidewater town. Willard was an ambitious risk-taker in the food brokerage business; Lydia, a schoolteacher bent on social recognition. She educated the six children with a live-in tutor and servants and sent the girls to boarding school. With the instability of the market in 1916, Willard Rouse lost most of his business when he bought tomato futures and the price dropped. To make matters worse Willard had already taken two mortgages on Brooklets. Several years later, at age four, Jimmy contracted polio that left him completely paralyzed. Spinal taps and months of therapy at Johns Hopkins Hospital in Baltimore started him on a painful journey of recovery.

Brooklets is the 3-story manor house in Easton, Maryland, where Jim Rouse was born. Shortly after both parents died, the estate was taken in bankruptcy. The home later burned (as shown) and was demolished.——Historical Society of Talbot County

After a long heart illness, Lydia died February 17, 1930. Plagued by cancer and dwindling finances, Willard followed on July 31, leaving Jim Rouse, the youngest child, an orphan at sixteen. Two months later, debt and bankruptcy claimed the eight-bedroom house, garden and stable. Partially destroyed by fire in the late 1920s or early 1930s, Brooklets was later demolished.

By then several of the other Rouse siblings had married and left Easton. Jim's older brother Bill (Willard, Jr.) remained, dedicated to looking after him. The boys first went to live with a married sister in town, later moving into a rooming house. "At Easton High School Jim became president of both his class and student council, edited a paper called the *Belfry Bat*, and belonged to the basketball and track teams," according to the 1982 *Current Biography*.

At graduation the sponsoring brothers and sisters considered him too young for college, so Jim Rouse was sent for a year to The Tome School, a private Maryland prep school on the banks of the Susquehanna River.

At the end of the year, he drove with friends to California in a Model T Ford. Then, with financial help from a friend's father, he went on to Hawaii by ship to live with his oldest sister and her naval officer husband. After a year at the University of Hawaii, with stirrings of homesickness, he returned to spend a few months at the University of Virginia taking twenty-one credits during his first semester, but dropped out in March of the second semester (1933). The Great Depression brought him to Baltimore to work parking cars at the St. Paul Garage although he didn't know how to drive, so his boss taught him. His workweek was fifty-four hours and the pay $13.50.

"In those days you could attend law school after only two years of college," Jim wrote seemingly apologetic in his unpublished autobiography. Attending part-time, he graduated from the University of Maryland law school in the spring of 1937 with an LL.B. degree. After cramming during the summer, he took the bar exam in November and passed with the second highest score in the state.

In 1934, while finishing law school at night, he quit the garage and went to work as a legal clerk with the Federal Housing Administration in Baltimore. Then, a year and a half later, with the encouragement of his friend and mentor, Guy T. O. Hollyday, Jim joined Title Guarantee and Trust Company and organized a mortgage department. His salary was $3,600 and his ambitious character began to materialize.

In June 1939 at age twenty-four, Jim started a mortgage banking business with a partner, wealthy Philadelphian and Princeton grad, Hunter Moss, two years his senior. Capitalization in the form of $20,000 came from Moss's sister, Sara Larrimer, and a personal friend, Willard Fowlke. "We flipped a coin to see whose name would come first; the other would be chairman and chief executive officer," Rouse later wrote. "Hunter won the flip and the Moss-Rouse Company opened for business in humble offices on Charles Street.

"Moss-Rouse was a mortgage banker operating as a correspondent for insurance companies, savings and commercial banks and other large financial institutions," Jim wrote. "We concentrated on FHA residential loans, a new but fast-growing part of the mortgage business. Continental American Life was our first big client and was quickly followed by Connecticut General in 1940."

Jim added: "In May [3] of 1941, after a courtship that lasted more than three years, I married Elizabeth 'Libby' [Jameson] Winstead, an attractive Baltimore girl.

"I was a customer parking my car at the St. Paul Garage when we first met," recalled Libby.

December 7, 1941, made everyone rethink his future. Because fourteen Moss-Rouse principals were under thirty, it was obvious that a provision would have to be made to keep the company operating while they went off to war. Jim and

Hunter hired forty-five-year-old Harry Batchelor, a trusted friend to manage their finance business, together with a board of directors that included Hunter Moss's father, Frank. Hunter enlisted in the Marines. Initially, Jim was temporarily deferred from military induction because of the pending birth of their first child (July 4, 1942).

Rouse had been in the Naval Reserves. He got into the Navy AVS program set up by Admiral Jack Towers to attract and train especially well-qualified men into the Naval Air Service. Rouse wrote: "As I had a law degree and had developed my own business, I was accepted. We began with ninety days of intensive training at Quonset Point, Rhode Island…. I was sent to gunnery school in Jacksonville, Florida." Then Jim was shipped to the Pacific as gunnery officer in a patrol squadron of PBY amphibian aircraft at Kaneohe Bay, Oahu, in the Hawaiian Islands. Later he was promoted to head the personnel office of Fleet Air Wing II, then soon made personnel officer of the Commander, Air Force, Pacific Fleet and transferred to Ford Island in the middle of Pearl Harbor. As a young naval officer, Rouse cut a handsome figure. He was nearly six feet tall weighing only 170 pounds and looked great in his custom-tailored uniforms, especially wearing his cap that covered his prematurely balding head.

Rouse was assigned to Quarters 114, a homey three-bedroom bungalow with other leaders in the AVS program including "Wing" Pepper who would become CEO of Scott Paper Company; Harry Hollins, future founder of the Institute for World Order; Dick Emory, later attorney general of Maryland; Augie Belmont, managing director of Dillon, Reed; Sam Neel, a Washington lawyer; and Lee Loomis, a Wall Street financier who didn't actually live at 114, but was an important part of the group as was Oakley Thorne who brought deep pockets to play poker, gin and bridge.

Jim was embarrassingly good with cards, amazing for a man who condemned casino gambling later in his career. "I won most of the time," wrote Rouse, "often a hundred dollars a night. I never drew a dollar of my regular service pay for the entire two years I was in the Pacific. I lived off my card-game winnings." He could add those to the six to eight hundred dollars he won on the ten-day voyage coming to the islands as well as high stakes poker at the BOQ [Bachelor Officers' Quarters].

After nearly three years of service, Jim, Hunter and the other principals returned to Moss-Rouse Company, pleasantly surprised to find it still profitable. Over the next decade with a high volume of conventional, FHA and GI mortgage loans, the firm flourished. In 1952, Moss-Rouse set up a small research department, called Metropolitan Research and Development, to help do a better job of evaluating prospective projects and obtaining financing. Two years later, Jim brought in his older brother, Bill, as a vice president. It was in this period that Moss began showing signs of discontent. The hiring of Bill may have been perceived as a threat.

Jim called his brother a master salesman having sold life insurance, Ford cars, Fuller Brushes and fire extinguishers. He immediately put him in charge of a new department set up to lease retail space in future shopping centers. Finally with Hunter Moss unhappy with the direction the company was taking, Rouse decided to buy out his partner. Jim's goal was to enter and expand into shopping center management and development. His first project was Mondawmin, followed by several other projects from Philadelphia to Austin, Texas. Then came The Village of Cross Keys.

Jim Rouse heard that the Baltimore Country Club was about to sell sixty-eight acres of its golf course along Falls Road. It was a rolling half-mile strip of land west of Roland Park and enclosed by the Jones Falls stream, Northern Parkway and, abutting at its southern extremity, a ragged parcel condemned three years earlier by the city to construct an I-83 interchange and a new high school complex. This was the opportunity Jim needed to build his first residential and commercial community and he asked the country club board if he could submit a proposal for development. A man who could charm, persuade and sell, Jim Rouse was confident that he could make The Village of Cross Keys something unique in urban living.

The history of Cross Keys Village and The Village of Cross Keys are forever entwined, far beyond their two villages, with the history of Baltimore and Maryland. And at times, too, the two men noted were sometimes overshadowed by strong women, black and white, who gave their support, leadership and counsel to the progress of the area.

1

Cross Keys Village, The Road and Falls

The first Cross Keys Village was located along both sides of Falls Road, just north of Coldspring Lane, at the time part of Baltimore County. It was named after the once-prominent Cross Keys Inn, built in the late eighteenth century on the west side of Falls Road opposite what is now CVS Pharmacy. The inn had been a place to entertain, lodge and feed the dusty and fatigued travelers of the road. The community surrounding the old hostelry was comprised mostly of African Americans, part of the freeborn settlements that once populated parts of Falls Road, principally at Cross Keys, Mt. Washington, Bare Hills and Shawan. While the Cross Keys area was once known as West Roland Park, it was listed as *Cross Keys Village* on early maps. Many residents simply called their community "The Road" or "The Falls Road," with an emphasis on *The.*

Cross Keys Village was probably patterned after the many mill towns that sprang up along rivers in colonial America. First someone wanted to be close to work and built a house, not much more then a shelter. Then others arrived and the second was built, then another and another until the settlement deserved the name of village. Cross Keys consisted of clapboard bungalows with their gable ends facing Falls Road, sandwiched between Coldspring Lane and Hillside Road. Period maps show that the homes were first built on the east side, probably on land purchased from Richard J. Capron or the Ridgely family.

The "crossed keys" is a symbol of St. Peter and said to be guardian of the gate of heaven and the power on which all justice and mercy depend. The influence of the Catholic Church was such that many inns used religious references in their signboards. Historian William Hollifield offered the idea that the name of the Cross Keys Inn may have come from the town Cross Keys in Monmouthshire, northwest of Newport, England.

In 2003, a few of the Cross Keys Village homes are still standing among newer commercial buildings, but only on the east side of the road. To make room for the Baltimore Polytechnic Institute-Western High School complex and a highway entrance ramp, all Cross Keys homes on the west side of Falls were condemned and demolished in the fall of 1961. In the Sanborn-Perris map of 1901, there are seventy-six dwellings shown. Only eleven remain. Paul M. Johnson, 73, a former resident of the old Cross Keys Village, remembered most of the families who lived in the homes before they were razed. With the help of friends, he compiled the list of resident names found in the Appendix.

The following is from an article published in the Baltimore *Sun*, December 27, 1908 at about the time The Roland Park Company had begun developing its "Plat One" on the eastern side of Roland Avenue. Mrs. Charles Baker was one of the oldest residents in Cross Keys Village. She was the widow of a man who pastured his cows near the Jones Falls and owned the Cold Spring Dairy at the corner of Falls and Coldspring Lane. She is quoted here:

"There used to be a large grove of chestnut trees on the top of the [Roland Park] hill…here and there were patches of huckleberry and blackberry bushes. Set back in the trees was the [Hiram] Woods house. We always called it the Capron house because the Caprons owned it a long time, and the edge of the estate ran beyond where the Ridgewood road is now.

"The children of the neighborhood used to go up there and gather chestnuts, and it was a favorite picnic ground." Continuing her reminiscences, Mrs. Baker said: "Where the Roland Park spring house is now there used to be a great natural spring known far and wide in the locality around here as Rock Spring. It was a solid stream of water, as big around as my arm, that shot out of the rock five feet from the ground.

"There used to be a picnic ground around here [White Oak Grove] and some of the water was used by residents in Cross Keys.

"Long before Roland Park thought of coming into existence, the village of Cross Keys, which skirts the Jones Falls base of the eminence upon which the [P]ark is built, and is now given over chiefly to darkies, was living in quiet uninspiring fashion.

"Just when Cross Keys began nobody knows…. Probably the village sprang up coincidentally with Mount Washington (Washingtonville it was called then) and other little communities in the Jones Falls Valley, simply because it was near pure water and had good pastureland," said Mrs. Baker.

The early Falls Road—from Baltimore harbor to Pennsylvania—followed an Indian trail along Jones Falls and was a main route of transportation for the colonists. White adventurers began to create settlements near the river mouth and it was just a matter of time before its upstream waters were put to use powering grist mills. Baltimore became a major British colonization and the rivers brought great wealth for the few who set up industries particularly along the Jones Falls. Named for David Jones who in 1661 settled 380 acres of marshland along the eastern bank of its mouth, Jones Falls extended fourteen miles into the wild Greenspring Valley and became the principal water source for the early settlements.

The coming together of Native Americans and the invading Europeans intent on laying claim to land, furs and resources, clashed with predictable results. Tiny Baltimore Town was stockaded against raids from the north by marauding Senecas whose path traversed its western boundary. The tall, fierce Susquehannocks also engaged in warfare with tribes in the south of Maryland until defeated by the Iroquois with whom they later joined. After 1677 Indian raids became "more severe and devastating." They were known to hunt in areas between the Susquehanna and Potomac Rivers and settle temporarily in Rockland during the summer months, according to Tom Bruggman, an amateur historian. Peter Taylor, a resident of Roland Park whose home overlooks the eighteenth fairway, said that while putting an addition on his house, the bulldozer scrapings of the ground revealed blackened, circular fire pits and shards of pottery, formerly an Indian encampment.

Falls Road was first known as Tyson's Mill Road. As early as 1788, its right-of-way traversed the length of the Jones Falls Valley. However the route was dusty and often muddy in the warm rainy seasons and filled with deep frozen ruts in winter. After the port of Joppa Town in Baltimore County lost its political stature to Baltimore Town in 1768, Falls Road became an even more important route for access to the growing number of mills, foundries, country farmers and post service. And to compete with the northbound toll routes on Reisterstown (Hookstown) and York Roads, local business interests proposed making the Falls Road a toll road. The surface of the "Falls Turnpike Road" was to be forty-feet wide, crowned and covered with fourteen inches of crushed stone. Costing $7,500 a mile, four-and-a-half miles were opened in 1807, though tolls weren't collected for several years because the road was still not complete.

At the time, it was predicted that the enterprise would be very lucrative. The Falls Road had three tollgates, one near North Avenue, one at Cross Keys Village and another 4/10th of a mile south of Rockland Mills where the Falls goes under the road. The toll keeper's house still stands there on the east side of the road. Tollgates were added as users found ways of shortcutting the road. Early accounts say there was a gneiss quarry every half-mile along the Falls Road and it was hoped that the heavy loads and wide wheels of the quarry wagons would help maintain the crushed stone surface.

The tollgate shed at Cross Keys Village stood next to the white clapboard and stone inn. But it was the two big crossed keys hanging from the inn's signboard that told tired travelers they could soon stretch their legs, wash, get something to eat and drink, and rest their horses. Heading into bustling Baltimore Town during different eras, teams of farm wagons and Conestogas were filled with tobacco, cotton sail cloth, seine netting, hay, grain, produce, butter and eggs, plaster and flour and drawn by four or six horses. Some would deliver their goods to wholesale markets and hotels while others went to meet ships at the Calvert Street Wharf. Once unloaded at the docks, they would pick up imported products such as silks, raw cotton, lumber, groceries, tropical fruits and dry goods. Then heading north from Baltimore, teams followed the Falls along the east bank dispensing goods to the local industries and settlements and on to Hanover, Carlisle and York, Pennsylvania. It is also believed Falls Road had been used to roll hogsheads of tobacco to Inspection House on Charles Street and on to the warehouses in Spring Gardens on the harbor and the Baltimore docks for exporting.

Stagecoaches, single riders carrying mail, and herds and flocks of livestock moved along the same country road. The forty-five-mile trip to York would take longer than a day. Tolls were charged by the number of horses, wheels and people. Wide rimmed (four inches and over) wheels cost less because they didn't dig into the packed gravel surface as much as would thin rims, which could require road repairs. A wagon with two horses and four wheels had to pay a toll of 2 1/2 cents per mile. The road curved back and forth over the Jones Falls. From Rockland Mills north, it continued as a free unsurfaced road.

Richard Caton, another son-in-law of Charles Carroll of Carrollton, and president of the Falls Turnpike Company, wanted the county to extend the road nine miles to the Pennsylvania line costing $38,000. That progress would have brought the traffic adjacent to Caton's Brooklandwood estate (now St. Paul's School) and his limekiln furnace and flourmill, lowering his transportation costs. The county refused his request.

With the arrival in 1829 of the Baltimore & Susquehanna Railroad (later to become the Northern Central Railway) and the Parkton local of the Pennsylvania Railroad in the mid-19th century, the inns, taverns, blacksmith shops and four-wheeled wagons began to fade from the Jones Falls Valley. However, the Cross Keys Inn survived the reduction of commercial turnpike traffic and actually thrived as a tavern supported by the villagers, mill and foundry workers at nearby Woodberry, and quarrymen along the turnpike who stopped after work for drinking and sometimes disorderly activity. As transportation methods improved, city folks flocked to the tavern for weekend entertainment. Over the long history of the inn, there have even been hints of ladies of the evening frequenting the upper floors of the establishment.

Free black men and women and families began to move into the small villages along the Falls. During the late 1700s, a few black men were employed by Quaker-owned businesses and manufacturers. Withstanding the heat of forge furnaces was thought to be a characteristic of people of African descent. In addition to the inn and homes, Cross Keys Village at its peak was comprised of two African American churches, a small hospital (probably a doctor's office), three grocery stores, a dairy, a cafe, a park (White Oak Grove) and a public school for "colored" children.

For greater profitability, many flour mills along the Falls were later converted into cotton mills and the old water wheels began to power looms instead of mill stones. Entrepreneur Horatio Nelson Gambrill built the Druid Mill in 1865, expanded and operated it with his sons until his death in 1880. Through the Gambills' efforts, Baltimore supplied fifty percent of the cloth needed for ship sails, ropes and netting around the world. From the city wharves, twenty railway trains a day laden with raw cotton made the run to the mill, then returned with finished products. Horatio's father, John Gambrill, owned land upstream on the Falls where the Cylburn mansion now stands. At one time, he also was proprietor of the Cross Keys Inn, later managed by his nephew, Perry Knight.

On March 2, 1878, the school house in Cross Keys Village "took fire," the Baltimore *Sun* reported "and would have been destroyed but for the exertions of neighbors. The damage was slight." This was probably the first of two schoolhouses in Cross Keys Village, and it was located on the east side of the road, later becoming a lodge hall, and then the Falls Road AME Church.

Top, Falls Road AME *first started in a private home on Falls Road, then it took over the first colored school, left, by then abandoned. Right, a new stucco facade was added. Bottom,* The church choir stands in front and *includes* left to right, *Samuel Brown, Laurinda Lee, William Gary, Hampton Green, Bernice Hawkins Copeland, George N. Brown, Beulah Scott, Aquilla Scott, Marie Harrady, Don Turner, Edith Merritt and Sadie Turner.*

Most of the five hundred people who lived in Cross Keys were African American. In later years, many worked as cooks, butlers, chauffeurs, gardeners, domestics, and even salad makers, for the prosperous in Roland Park. But some, with years of entrepreneurial spirit and accumulated wealth, ran their own businesses, prospered and sent their children to college and grandchildren into the professions.

In those early days, not all the African Americans resided along Falls Road. There were several homes folded into ridges of the original Harper estate that is now the west side of Roland Park. Aunt Lucy Hoe was part of such an enclave "in back of the old water tower" [now the site of the former Girls Latin Gym]. It is said that her husband bought the valuable piece of ground "for a song." She may have been related to Charles Grandison Hoes, Jr., who in the mid-1850s settled Hoes Heights, a black community across Coldspring to the south. For many years, Aunt Lucy served the Fendall family who had owned the Woodlawn estate before it was purchased by the Caprons and finally the Roland Park Company. Mrs. Frances Thwaites Cockey Fendall was a direct descendant of Charles Ridgely. There were also two homes of Negroes near Coldspring Lane that "marred the beauty of the perspective Park" and "were moved back bodily some distance from the property line of the Park with the permission of the owners."

Where Hillside Road zigzags east near Ridgewood Road in Roland Park, there was an acre of land owned by "two or three Negro families and occupied by their small shacks and the smallest of burying grounds." The parcel had been given them by descendants of the Harper family. When [Hiram] Woods had purchased the larger surrounding land, he "offered in a spirit of liberality, to transplant the group—houses, burying ground and all—to holdings in Cross Keys; but the humble proprietors clung tenaciously to the soil on which they were planted, and refused to be moved despite all persuasion." The miniature settlement continued…even after the Roland Park Company [having organized in July 1891], had acquired the land." By 1895, however, it had been reduced to a single household consisting of a ninety-year-old woman and a son of seventy. "In the great blizzard of that year these old people were quite forgotten for several days and were rescued just in time to save their lives, for they had been without food for forty-eight hours." Several years later both the woman and her son were dead. The story was reported in the Baltimore *Sun*.

To give an idea of how Roland Parkers saw the adjacent Cross Keys Village and its African American inhabitants, research produced a condescending description of what a fictitious traveler saw of the village as he rode north out of Hampden on the No. 25 Falls Road trolley. The following passage came from the official organ of the Roland Park Civic League called *Roland Park Review*, dated January 1919. It was written in the style of B. Latrobe Weston, former editor of the *Review* and grandson of Benjamin H. Latrobe, the great English-born architect of many outstanding structures including the U. S. Capitol's north and south porticoes, the Catholic Cathedral in downtown Baltimore, and the classic dairy building once located on the property of Robert Goodloe Harper's Oakland. Weston wrote:

> "As the traveler on the Falls Road trolley crosses the limits of the city and descends the incline to Cold Spring Lane he sees ahead on the summit of the hill to the right an imposing group of fine mansions, whose commanding position dominates the landscape.
> "Among the rounded contours of the intervening slope he notes also an irregular assemblage of dwellings, barns and outhouses, which straggles up

toward the hedge bounding the grounds above. The stately residents of the hilltop are those whose fronts border upon Ridgewood Road, the westernmost avenue of the suburb of Roland Park; the unpretentious buildings on the declivity belong to the adjacent village of Cross Keys.

"As the baron of old looked down from his castle walls upon vassal hamlet huddling under the hillside, so the dweller on Ridgewood Road looks from his lofty terrace upon the holdings of his humbler neighbor of Cross Keys…the very heart and center [of which] was the ancient inn…which until a few weeks ago was still standing.

"With these [few] exceptions the inhabitants of Cross Keys are mainly of African decent. Gardening is the principal occupation—that simple rustic art first practiced by Adam, the progenitor of the race, and ever since held to be a respectable and honorable calling. The neighboring grounds of Roland Park offer the necessary field for employment. As an adjunct to gardening, there is also furnace-tending, a most happy combination, the two kinds of service being seasonal; the former being necessary in summer, the latter in winter. The women of the village also find occupation in Roland Park in the way of washing and domestic service. A most fortunate relationship is thus established between the two communities; each is dependent upon the other, and it would be difficult to imagine how either could be comfortable or prosperous alone."

During the summer months, those owners of the "fine mansions" on Roland Park's Ridgewood Road were bothered by mosquitoes. It was thought that many of the creatures were rising from Cross Keys Village, just below the brow of the hill, that the bothersome insects were apparently spawned in the leaky rainwater barrels used by the residents for doing laundry. By this time, Latrobe Weston had become secretary of the Civic League and taken on the task of ridding Roland Park of flies and mosquitoes. Every pond, stable, ditch and garbage receptacle and even inside toilet tanks were suspect breeding chambers in Roland Park. Here is yet another descriptive passage from the pen of Weston and published in an earlier Roland Park newsletter, this one titled "Cross Keys in the Line of Progress," dated May 1915. The richness of the black vernacular might have been acceptable in Victorian Roland Park, but the prejudice they embody clearly would *not* be acceptable today. For historical purposes, former African American residents of Cross Keys Village felt it was important to include these passages.—Author

Eddie Scott gets ready for a fast getaway in the back of his Bare Hills home. The rain barrel provided water for washing and laundry. The galvanized tubs under the porch were used for Saturday night baths.—Marie Scott Brown

"Cross Keys may be said to have had improvement thrust upon it, as the new [rain] barrels are a largess from Roland Park, and, while accepted with the natural readiness attached to things bestowed without cost, are regarded as with somewhat incredulous incomprehension as to the function they are to perform. 'Is dat so?' said a respectable darkey, whose whitening wool betokened advancing years, and whose eyes evidenced a slowly dawning understanding of the newly acquired apparatus. 'Dey breeds mosquitoes, does dey?' [referring to the old-time rain barrels]. 'Well I never thought of dat.'

"When the matter was explained to another citizen (colored like all the population, with few exceptions), he agreed that 'mosquitoes was bad to bother you on the porch, about as bad as chintzes,' which, he said were truly malevolent!

"It is all well enough for Roland Park to ask incredulously about rain barrels, as though unable to imagine what purpose such receptacles serve. Roland Park with its up-to-date water supply, knows little of old-time, age-long methods; nor is it interested extensively in the washing industry, which is flourishing in Cross Keys.

"Cross Keys with *no* water supply, washes probably more clothes than Roland Park, and rain water is better, from the clothes-washing viewpoint, than Roland Park water. It is softer and better suited to the purpose. Consequently, most families in Cross Keys operate one or more barrels. They provide liquid of the best washing quality, and they save laborious trips without number to the spring. The by-product—mosquitoes—has not come within the Cross-Keysan mental horizon, and would have been treated with contempt if it had.

"Now, however, that something new and improved is to be had, and had gratis for the asking, suspicion is overcome and demand is eager. Families near the spring that did not support a barrel, want one, and families that had one, with possibly an ancient wreck in addition for an occasional auxiliary supply, ask for two good new ones.

"The new barrels, set upon substantial supports and provided with brass spigots, are prominent features in the Cross-Keysan backyard landscape, and rather throw surrounding objects into the shade by force of contrast. The recent rains have filled them to overflowing and it is sheer pleasure to turn the spigots and see the limpid stream flow out. We think washday after their installation must have been a gala occasion, and that valuable time was probably lost in comparing notes of the new apparatus across fences. Meanwhile, Ridgewood Road should rejoice in the prospect of a mosquitoeless summer, so far as human foresight can insure it."

Today, all of the rain barrels are gone, together with most of the village, replaced by commercial establishments. Now the greasy odor of fast food restaurants along Falls Road wafts upward to the folks above on Ridgewood Road. The mosquitoes, for the most part, have been controlled.

Heading north along the Falls Road Turnpike, horse, carriage and two gentlemen are leaving the No. 25 trolley car in the dust at the top of the hill. In this 1906 photograph, the Roland Park cricket barn can be seen next to the road, as well as mansions on the ridge above. To the right is the golf course that would become The Village of Cross Keys.—Maryland Historical Society

Here are some more of Weston's writings about Cross Keys Village in the April, 1909, issue of *Roland Park Review*. It was titled: "Cross Keys: A Near Neighbor" and has been edited to eliminate the redundancies from what Mr. Weston had written both in his *Evening Sun* newspaper column and in earlier Roland Park musings…

"The latter settlement [Cross Keys Village] drags its length in an aimless, purposeless sort of way along both sides of Falls Road from Cold Spring Lane, perhaps a quarter of a mile northward. Houses most varied in size and character are spaced at unequal intervals. On the left [west] is a single row only, for back of these a stream flows through a pretty piece of meadow land—the same which lower down traverses the southern reaches of the golf course and emits finally into Jones Falls. On the right [east], narrow lanes give access to dwellings on the higher levels, and wander about with a delightful lack of system in a maze of sheds and backyards. Gnarled and shaggy trees—oaks, poplars, willows and ailanthus—are interspersed at odd places and corners. One comes unexpectedly across stone walls supporting terraces of earth as one climbs higher, until at length an intervening field is crossed and one looks back from the tall hedge which marks the line dividing from Roland Park on the summit. From this point of vantage the little village is seen a confused mass of roofs and pointed gables…

"Yet, in point of view of length of days Cross Keys is far more entitled to consideration, and has, in fact, a right to regard its near companion as a very parvenu in the select society of older towns. For the beginning of Cross Keys was laid some hundred years ago, when Washingtonville was a small community clustering about its mill, and its present successor, Mt. Washington, existed only in the hazy future.

"In the days when railroads were unknown and the teaming from the upper county as an important matter, [the Cross Keys Inn] was a thriving hostelry. On the signboard displayed before its hospitable door were depicted two large keys, crossing each other, to describe, as may be imagined, the security of lodging to be obtained under its roof. By the translation of this pictorial insignia into words of actual speech, resulted in time the name by which the surrounding village became known—Cross Keys. The title is euphonious, and has much to recommend it.

"Closely connected with the inn at this time was the enclosure on the opposite side of the road, which is still known as "White Oak Grove," the words appearing above the entrance gateway…. A few dwellings have also been erected in the grove, and the great oaks which once looked down on mirthful celebrations now behold only the quiet operations of domestic industry.

"A prominent resident is Anton Spath, the elder, who is, in fact, the patriarch of the settlement, as his years now number more than the allotted three score and ten. Mr. Spath's home is about at the center of the village—a substantial building whose grounds are raised several feet above the level of the roadway, the earth being sustained in place and protected on the vertical outside edge by a rough masonry wall. Here on fine days the old man may be seen walking about, with the aid of a stick, in his pleasant yard among his evergreens and flowers. A large part of the land on which stands the homes of his neighbors belongs to Mr. Spath. He is also owner of a quarry high up on the hill in the rear of his dwelling, whence has come much of the stone wherewith the smooth roads of the Park have been surfaced.

"The principal one of the three stores which the village supports is carried on by Anton Spath, son of Mr. Spath the elder, as the name of the former, appearing in large letters above an unpretentious building on the west side of the roadway, indicates. There is an active trade in general merchandise, groceries, clothing, household utensils and nondescript articles of all sorts and varieties."

Latrobe Weston again goes on to talk about the fortunate relationship between Roland Park and Cross Keys:

"That the mutual relationship is a profitable one on the Cross Keysan side is evidenced by the handsome dwelling lately erected by Samuel Brown, which, with its generally pleasing aspect of freshness and newness, is a conspicuous object on the east side of the roadway. Also Cross Keys is no standstill place, but is growing. Several additional cottages have been erected within the last year, and there is a clearly apparent tendency to build up the higher limits of the hillside in the direction of the Roland Park line.

"Cross Keys has a church, and also a schoolhouse. The county rents the latter building from its owners, a society known as the Lodge of the Seven Wise Men. Just what are the aims of this organization is known only to the members; from the name, however, one would argue something very deep and secret and mysterious.

"Cross Keys is not troubled with esthetic ideals, nor are its methods even up to date in the exacting modern sense of the term. Questions that disturb the consciousness of Roland Park, such as "removal of trash from lanes" or "better receptacles for garbage and ashes," are not subjects of discussion at town meetings. Even so obtrusive a matter as "the unnecessary display of family wash" passes unheeded, and on almost every day of the week the scraggly and attenuated encasements of arms and legs may be observed in the backyards, flapping fantastically in the agitating air currents. After all, as to the last, are not the Cross Keysans more philosophic and reasonable than their near neighbors? Carlyle has clearly shown in his immortal work, Sartor Resartus, that it is the clothes that make the man. Why, then, should we be ashamed of the necessary nether investiture of our persons?

"In Cross Keys it is the practical side of life that is prominent. Two or three of the small holdings are separated from the road by a border of hedge, and have grass and flowers in season, but most of the villagers are concerned with questions of subsistence, and have little time for considerations of adornment. Close beside Roland Park, with all the conveniences of modern improvement, stands Cross Keys, practicing indifference the methods of primitive simplicity."

Weston's writings certainly offer valuable descriptions of Cross Key's historical importance, but his insidious and obnoxious style are shocking and not appropriate today. It should be added that all the shortcomings noted in his references to Cross Keys: trash in the lanes, displays of family wash, and mosquitoes had first been directed by Weston at the residents of Roland Park in earlier issues of the *Review* from which he resigned in 1912. He died at 81 on December 20, 1949.

2

Vital Family Community

As Cross Keys Village grew, it took on the aura of a strong family community. Virtually everyone knew everybody else. Some families bought their homes along Falls Road, others moved from one property to another as better rents and more space became available. But most of the people remained in their comfortable setting from the times when the village was considered "country." Then at the end of the nineteenth century, its future was tied to the establishment of Roland Park and its need for low cost labor.

The residence at 4713 Falls Road is believed to be one of the oldest (c. 1844) still standing on the east side of the Cross Keys community. It was the home for six generations of Scotts, one of several African American names that was prominent in the area. Brown, Bond, Hawkins, Phillips, Harvey, Johnson, Parker, Yates, Chaney, McBride and Young were others. Anthony "Tony" Parker grew up in the 4713 home. His grandmother was Edith Scott who married Bartholomew "Barnamus" Parker, a black Jew. His father was Arthur Grafton Parker, his mother Shirley Clemons. Tony, a mortgage banker and his wife, Holly, a Realtor, own 4713 and several of the remaining dwellings, including their residence also on the east side of Falls Road.

The attractive clapboard two-story at 4713 can still be seen today. "It first sprouted from a small house built by my great, great grandparents Rev. Edward W. Scott and his wife Henrietta," said Tony Parker. "Then my great grandfather, Simon P. Scott, Sr., and great uncles added more space on the first floor, and a second floor and veranda were raised and finally additions carried the home halfway through its deep narrow lot." There was even a separate house and garage built behind 4713, smack against the steep hill that rises to Roland Park. It took the address of 4715. "I always liked that pretty little place," said Parker, "even had a brick privy. Few people knew it was back there. Once I drove my late model car into the garage next to the place, but it was so small, I couldn't open my car door." After the little house was nearly destroyed by fire in the late '70s, what remained was given to Parker.

Top, *Anthony and Holly Parker are among the last to have lived on Falls Road in the old Cross Keys Village. Tony's roots can be traced to the slave Tobias.* Bottom, *One of the oldest homes still standing in Cross Keys Village (c. 1844) is the former Scott residence and store at 4713 Falls Road.*

At one time, the first floor front of 4713 doubled as a store run by Edith Scott Parker. "She was a wonderful person," said her cousin Marie Scott Brown. "There was nothing fake about Edith. But her sister Lydia was sort of a snob." Edith made clothes for the ladies of Roland Park and, at the store sold fresh produce, poultry, some meats and groceries. "It wasn't your modern Giant Food Market," laughed Holly Parker, who has been helping her husband record his extensive family lineage. "The store was a gathering place to get simple supplies and learn what was happening in the community," she said. Cross Keys Village was a tight little place in those days. There may have been pig troughs, chickens roaming, horses clopping to and from the stable near Hillside Road, but it was a family neighborhood of kids, grandparents and hard-working parents. Vertelle Hawkins Hall, a former resident said every adult knew all the children, looked after them and helped raise them. "It takes a village," she smiled. Only a few families moved away from the security of Cross Keys. Tony Parker's uncle Calvin "Billie" Scott moved to Arizona. "My family was famous for its allergies," he said.

In wintertime, the village became a more quiet, deliberate place. Inhabitants stayed by their wood and coal stoves and pushed newspaper into the cracks to seal off the cold west winds that blew across the valley. When snows came, the children would burst outside to enjoy whatever sledding venture they could find. While organized coasting parties took place on a half-dozen closed streets in Roland Park, it was the two toboggan runs on the steep eighteenth fairway hill of the golf course that attracted most. On the top of country club hill, people were pressed against the steamy windows of the elegant clubhouse watching kids and over-the-hillers belly flopping or tobogganing on the freshly iced snow. There were single sleds and double-deckers. At night maintenance people were using the summer sprinkler system to wet down the toboggan runs to help them freeze. A big pile of hay at the bottom was supposed to stop the bobsled. In Roland Park, toboggan sledding began in 1905, when snow was hauled to the eighteenth fairway for the slide.

Charles Seabreeze, who used to live at 4682 Falls Road, was sledding down the club hill when somehow he got sidetracked and went over what he called a "ski jump." Whatever it was, it took him high above the crowd. "The people looked like they were this small," he beamed holding his thumb and forefinger two inches apart. Unfortunately, over the years, two sledders were killed on the hills. One ran into a pipe and another a guy wire. Winter sports for Roland Parkers included skating on the pond once located on the lower golf course south of the tenth hole. Nearby was a small house with a warm stove for changing footwear.

It took Cross Keys kids longer to get ready for a trip down Hillside Road. They had to build a sled or clean up an old Flexible Flyer from cluttered basements. "We used to start at the top," said June Hawkins Randall, "and come rattling down in a flash! We relied on someone standing at Falls Road to give us the signal to stop or cross over and continue onto the golf course below. I mean it was the best sled ride in the world! When the night of sledding was over," she said, "a Cross Keys grandmother or mother would serve hot chocolate and baked dough with sugar on top that we called cinnamon buns before heading back home at 4656 Falls Road."

Ann Gaskins Carter once lived at 4682 Falls Road. She and her six brothers and sisters (Colleen, Howard, twins Alexander and Andrew, Pamela and Brenda) were born in the house, built by her grandfather, Franklin Jones. Ann was named after her grandmother, Annie Jones, whom she adored. "We did a lot together," she said. "We'd go shopping at the A&P market on 36th Street. In the spring we'd pick dandelions, blackberries and 'poke,' a leafy vegetable to cook and make salads. Sometimes for sodas and snacks, we'd go to Mr. Douglass's store. He was such a nice man. Yes indeed, yes indeed. Ummm. Other times we'd go to Miss Molly's, a white lady who ran a store on the other side of Coldspring Lane in Medfield Heights. We'd take her empty soda bottles and exchange them for candy."

As a child, Ann was shy and afraid of some of her neighbors like "Doc" and Bessie White. "They lived like hermits." she said. "We were afraid to walk past the White's house, and at night, you never went near it. The bus stopped right in front of their house so it made it scary to even wait for the bus.

"We were also afraid of the Simon Scotts. They lived in a big house across the street and we considered them rich folks. But, at the time, they weren't too nice to children. Oh, my goodness, yes. And unless you had business there, my goodness, we were so scared because he was so mean. Oh goodness. Mean!

"And you can imagine how scared we were when a knock came to our front door at two in the morning," she said. "It was Garland Crosby. As a child, he'd sleepwalk and there he was, asking if my brother could come out and play. My grandmother ran him home.

"Some folks on Falls Road didn't have electricity or phones," said Ann, "and there were the party-lines. We had indoor plumbing, a bathtub and electricity and a car. My grandparents weren't considered rich, but we were well off. They never drove, but my mother, an only child, had a car. She was the only sixteen-year-old black girl to have her own. My grandfather did landscaping work for the people in Roland Park and she was his chauffeur. And every Saturday, she'd take him to 36th Street to Good Ann's drug store. Every Saturday. Sometimes my brothers at ten or twelve would 'steal' the car and drive it around the alleys and back lot. Boys are different. I didn't get my license until I had my first job when I was nineteen. As a youth, I went to Morgan State, sang in the choir and enjoyed the life of a student.

"From the time I was very young, my grandmother would take us downtown to Brager-Gutman's to shop, especially at Easter and Christmas," said Carter. "We never had any problems trying on clothes and hats. In later life, I always attributed that to the fact grandmother always carried herself like a lady. Black families from other areas were sometimes discriminated against. I never felt any kind of rudeness—never called a nigger. Someone told me—probably my grandmother—if you carry yourself like a responsible person, you'll always be respected.

Marie Scott Brown disputed that. "If you were colored, you were colored," she said. "Bragers catered to the poor people and most colored people went there. They were always cheaper than other places, but we couldn't go to Hutzler's or Stewart's." These were the days of Jim Crow laws (enacted July 1, 1904) in Baltimore. "And I always sat in the rear of the street cars. O-h y-e-a," she said slowly, looking pensive. "It was a different life then." Then she looked up, almost startled, as she remembered something else. "Sandler's store would bring boxes of clothes in a truck to sell in colored neighborhoods. We didn't have to go downtown so it was better especially for those women with children," said Marie.

"When I was small and going to school 158, if it would snow," said Ann Carter, "some of us kids would take our bottles of milk outside at lunchtime and bury them in the snow. When they froze, they were like ice cream. I guess it reminded me of my mother, Sidna, who made snowballs and apples-on-a-stick and sold them from our front porch during the summer.

One of the rare photographs of the west side of Cross Keys Village, c. 1960.

"Some residents never knew the name of the settlement was Cross Keys Village," she said. "We called it Falls Road. It was like one big family. You knew everybody. If you lived there, you just stayed there. If my home and neighborhood were still there, I'd be there. Memories of those days bring tears to my eyes," said Carter.

Reita Bryant Carroll who used to live at 4686 Falls Road recalled her snowy adventure coming down the Belvedere Avenue (now Northern Parkway) hill when her friend Marge hit a hidden stump and flipped end-over-end. "We were so scared," she said. "We thought she was dead or something so we started home for help. Fortunately, like most kids, Marge got on her feet and started yelling at us for leaving her. We used to do some dumb things," said Reita, "like moving furniture from front porches to the golf course during Halloween. On 'moving night,' my father also did something dumb. He stretched a cable across the yard between the houses. When the kids started carrying away rockers and chairs, they hit the cable and were splayed all over the side lawn. I guess everyone learned a lesson because my father never had to pull that dangerous trick again. They were times I'll always remember. I was born on the west side of Falls Road, but we had to move when I was five to make room for the high schools and I was sad."

Danger was all a part of growing up particularly for Cross Keys boys. Garland Crosby remembers. "Several of us used to grab hold of a boxcar ladder on a slow freight and hold on until we got to Lake Roland. Now that was fun. And one summer, another boy and I ran away from home, went up to camp overnight at Texas, Maryland, but came home by train when we got tired and hungry," he said.

In his Sunday white suit, the last thing young Charley Seabreeze heard as he headed out to play was his mother's admonition not to get his church clothes dirty. He and his buddy sauntered over to the Jones Falls "just to look." Then they spotted a concrete mixing tub, upside down, along the shoreline. As they righted the heavy wooden box, they figured it would float like a boat, so putting their weight behind it, Charley and his buddy shoved and pulled it into the water and got in. Soon they were floating downstream. "Everything was fine until we started looking for something to paddle with, and then over we went," said Seabreeze. "My white suit was soaked, muddy and I had lost a shoe. When I got home, I can still see my angry mother reach out the door, snatched my arm and I practically flew inside."

"On really hot summer days," said Sharon McBride, "many kids went to swim at 'Leaches Beach,' near a deep hole in Jones Falls. Sharon says she remembers her grandmother talking at the kitchen table about how leaches from the slow moving stream would attach themselves to their bodies. "We'd have to sit on a rock and pick them off each other when we came out," she said. Crosby, 66, of the same generation as Sharon's mother, said the scene was hilarious, "all of us kids, covered with leaches and almost afraid to touch them, saying, "Oooo," and "aauug," as we flicked them off.

"Our parents didn't want us going in the Jones Falls," said Garland. "Besides the leaches, there was a big black slimy rock near the middle of a section of deep water. You had to be able to swim to 'Black Rock' if you were to be considered a good swimmer. It was your badge of honor," he said. Also in the summer, Garland nostalgically thought about catching bullfrogs along the many streams that ran through the golf course. "There were big carp in the golf course pond and we'd wade in and catch them by hand. Some were as long as my arm. Of course we'd have to keep an eye out for Scotty, the Baltimore Country Club's greens keeper. If he saw us, he'd yell and chase us, most often if we were looking for balls to sell back to golfers." Blacks were not allowed on the country club golf course, but several boys did get to caddie, and some learned to play golf. Back in the 1920s, Baltimore-bred Cab Calloway caddied at the Baltimore Country Club before going on to national fame as a singer and bandleader in the '30s and '40s. It was about that time that Thurgood Marshall was tending tables at the Gibson Island Club, long before rising to the Supreme Court.

"On the other side of Jones Falls was a nasty area our parents forbid us to go," said Garland Crosby. "We finally realized it was the septic pond for all of Roland Park." The sewers of Roland Park were once thought to be the most advanced in the country. At first Edward H. Bouton, developer of Roland Park, wanted to simply "conduct our sewerage into the Jones Falls," but his suggestion was turned down. So at the turn of the twentieth century, one of the leading sanitary engineers in the country, Colonel George E. Waring, Jr., was hired to design a modern septic system. It was thought to be so revolutionary that the Roland Park Company's sales department gave flushing demonstrations for perspective homebuyers.

There were actually two septic systems, one for storm water and the other for toilets and other household wastes. The sludge from the east side of the Park was pumped uphill through six-inch glazed tile sewer pipes across Roland Avenue, then together with all the waste on the west side was gravity fed down Hillside and Oakdale Roads to a large screened well just north of the old cricket field. Here the solids were filtered out and the liquid continued on through pipes under Falls Road, across the fields and *over* Jones Falls, finally being deposited in a ten-acre disposal field of sand separated into seven retention ponds.

Using hand rakes, operators would make certain the sewage percolated through the sand and into underlying perforated pipes from which the liquid portion was returned "pure, some said" to the Jones Falls. You can still see the remains of the disposal field, now an ugly marshy lagoon behind the city's "stump dump," off Old Coldspring Lane. The villages from Mt. Washington to Pikesville also disposed their waste in the same way with a septic system on the west side of Jones Falls downhill from the Cylburn mansion.

Around 1950, the Roland Park sewerage system was replaced by the addition of the Jones Falls interceptor pipe that was added along the side of the Falls carrying sewage from an ever-increasing geographic area to a new pumping station at Ash Avenue and Clipper Mill Road. This unit then pumps waste seven miles over land ridges to the Back River processing plant off Eastern Avenue.

The vinegar factory was another off-limits delight for the kids of Cross Keys. On the bank of the Jones Falls near Old Coldspring Lane, the late Bill Boykin and his family owned and operated the plant for a while. Bill's dad built the huge wooden fermenting tanks and he said the periodic flooding Jones Falls made their life miserable. The vinegar factory used to be the site of Melvale Distillery Co., makers of Melvale Pure Rye. Bill Boykin also said they had their own method for disposing waste, but at that time, it wasn't a concern for Cross Keys swimmers. "There was something there that attracted us to the factory," said Ann Carter. "Maybe it was because we were told never to go there. But we did. Maybe it was because you could always smell the pungent odor of the vinegar and that was a constant reminder," she added. And malodorous scents also arose from the dump that the city created in back of the west side of the village. John McBride said, "It was like a landfill behind the portable classrooms. There were always fires in there."

"We used to go to the dump and play," said Ann Carter. "Once I slipped—it had steep sides—and I fell into all that glass, metal debris and smoldering mess. I still have scars on my leg to prove it," she said.

"We boys organized a club called the Bar 20," said Garland Crosby. "It was just an excuse for all of us to do the misdeeds that children do, so I won't get into that. Falls Road was our playground. All of us went to the same schools, traveled the same streetcars and buses. There we would be, all lined up along the road ready to board the trolley. Those early times and friends are some of my best memories. And even today, our generation and our children remain close even though we're spread out all over the place."

Greasing the tracks was a trick played by youngsters to watch the wheels spin as the trolley tried to get up a hill. And yes, Tony Lee was one of those kids we remember who pulled the electric pole off the overhead wire of the trolley car so the motorman or conductor had to get out and place the pulley carefully back on the wire. Tony went one better. He tied a rope from a front door of a neighbor on Falls Road, then to the rope on the trolley catcher. "When the car started, it pulled the door off the house," he said, and the rest of the story was lost in the laughter of Tony and his friends.

Charley McBride told a story about a snake that Delores Silva didn't want to hear. She's deathly afraid of them. "As a child we'd be playing in the woods," said Delores, "and someone yelled 'There goes a snake!' And the other kids said if you'd run a crooked path, the snake couldn't catch you. I never saw a snake, but from that time on, I've been terrified just to hear the word 'snake.' I even talked to a therapist about it, but he said the only way I could conquer my fear was to get in a room with a snake."

Or, Delores could go blackberry picking with Charley McBride. "We used to take a pot into the woods where the expressway is now." said McBride. "Once I had my pot near full of berries and put it down. I was always told *never* put your pot down in the woods. When I picked it up, it was fuller than when I put it down. There was a black snake curled up in the midst of the warm berries."

The stories from Cross Keys Village are many. Tony Parker's great grandparents, Rachel and Simon Scott, Sr., lived at 4713 Falls Road before the Civil War and are said to have been part of the "underground railroad," hiding escaped slaves in secret rooms in the attic and basement. In Maryland, a slave could cross the Mason-Dixon line after a night or two of careful traveling. Or, he could sail the Chesapeake into the mouth of Jones Falls, spend the night at an early Orchard Street Church, then take to the rutty Falls Road heading north to Harrisburg and the Susquehanna, go up-river to the West Branch, and west to the confluence of Pine Creek to northern Pennsylvania. Finally he could go on to New York to cross the Niagara River into Canada. "By 1860 there were 60,000 blacks in Upper Canada alone, of whom 45,000 were fugitive slaves," says Winks' *Blacks in Canada*. Of course there were dozens of other paths to freedom.

Besides the North Star, moss on trees, mountain ranges and streams indicating directions, there were secret devices used to help slaves find food, clothing and safe houses provided by free blacks and sympathetic whites. On their long odyssey north, tired and weary slaves were signaled by candles in attic windows, spirituals, bird calls, church bells, single code words and symbols drawn in the dirt. Often the signal code to show a willingness to feed and hide slaves was a "log cabin" pattern quilt hung from the fence, window or wash line. "Its traditional red square center [for the fireplace] was changed to black on the signal quilt," said Tom Bruggman, a psychologist who owns the restored Rockland tavern on Old Court Road at Falls Road.

Gladys-Marie Frey was one of the first to suggest that a log cabin quilt with a black center was a signal on the "underground railroad." The square spiral design first appeared in the 1840s at a time when the slaves were increasingly escaping their plantations. However, black fabric for the center square wasn't commercially available until the last decade of the nineteenth century. More likely, the "black" was a dark indigo blue. In those days, indigo-dyed cloth fashioned into wearing apparel was known as "black clothes."

Tony Harper, remembering the words of his great grandparents, believes there are secret niches in other Falls Road homes for hiding escaped slaves. Historian Jerry Hynson says when he lived at 4710 Falls Road in the village, there was a closet on the first floor under the stairs where there was a trap-door in the floor and a hole below, not really a basement. "Maybe just a root cellar," suggested Garland Crosby.

Although Maryland, as a border state, dealt with a high incidence of runaway slaves, the problem clearly worsened in the late 1840s. Ralph Clayton, author of three books on Maryland slaves, estimated the weekly value of fugitive slaves lost from the border counties in Maryland was about $10,000 by the spring of 1850. Advertisements offering rewards for runaways ran almost daily. And there were stories written in the news columns. This one is from the *Charlestown Maryland News*, September 20, 1855:

> "Stampede...a regular stampede of Negroes was made from this neighborhood on Saturday night last. They were ten in number. They took with them three horses and a double carriage belonging to Ed Ringgold's estate, and a carriage belonging to John Greenwood. They were all valuable Negroes, and it is to be hoped will be recovered. Up to the present time, however, nothing has been heard of them."

Not all slaves headed for escape beyond the Maryland-Pennsylvania border. Fugitives also fled to the cities in an attempt to blend in with the rest of the free black community. Baltimore was a principal destination. By 1810, it contained the largest numbers of free blacks of any city in the slave states. The fact that slaves and free blacks lived together in Baltimore was not unusual. It evolved as a result of a complex system of labor and management. Some slaves were hired out by their masters. Others, including free blacks, were indentured to whites for a "term of years" in the hope that the owner could provide better training, particularly for youngsters. Some city slaves who were given permission by their owners to live in their own rented apartments in back-alleys. This arrangement cut down food and clothing costs for the owner, and had a major benefit for the slaves beside their frail sense of freedom. It encouraged a secret word-of-mouth network to aid runaways. At the time, kidnapping of free blacks was made a serious crime. In the past they could be taken from the streets, with or without freedom passes, and shipped to the daily auction in Richmond, Virginia.

Tony Parker also remembers his parents talking about Prohibition in the early '20s. "White people from Hampden used to visit my aunt and uncle's tavern, which was then located on the empty lot next to the north side of CVS Pharmacy. The revenuers never cared much for venturing into our area in those days." And fear cut both ways. When Tony was a youngster, he went to the mostly white St. Thomas Aquinas School at Roland and 37th. He would run to and from school, always fearful that the white boys were laying in wait for him. Some years later when he met one of the grown "white kids," the young man asked,

"Why'd you always run? We weren't going to beat you up, we just wanted to ask you to play baseball with us."

Sharon McBride had to run through the mostly white Hampden, too. "The white kids would carry empty tin cans with jagged tops that they'd lunge at us little kids to cut our legs," she said. "But to balance out, there was always retribution when they came through Cross Keys."

Sharon loved to hear the stories told by the elders in her family. "My mother told me a story about how, as a child, she followed her four brothers into the woods where the I-83 expressway is now. They didn't want a girl to tag along, so they tied her to a tree. Toward evening when the boys came home, my grandmother asked 'Where's Elsie?' They had to go back and get her and they really got into trouble for that." Still, Sharon talks about the closeness of her family and friends. "At Christmas time there would be carolers walking and singing in front of every house in the village. Someone always served cocoa, cookies and eggnog."

One of the focal centers of Cross Keys Village was the Tyson African Union Methodist Protestant Church that was located, until the turn of this century, next to the north side of ManorCare Health Center. The church could have been named after the earliest name of the road or nearby mill. Or the land could have been given to the church by the Tyson family, Quakers who had empathy with local blacks. Most likely it was named for Elisha Tyson, a wealthy white miller in Woodberry who in 1789 helped found the state's first abolitionist society, also the African Academy school and, in 1818, set up a dispensary providing free medical care for the poor.

According to former residents, the Tyson AUMP Church's parishioners were mainly Scott family descendants. In fact it was locally referred to as "The Scott Church." It was founded in 1866 and, at its 30th Anniversary celebration, Rev. Edward W. Scott was pastor. He died sitting in bed November 20, 1919, at his home at 323 (earlier number), now 4703 Falls Road. He is buried in the cemetery of the Colored Methodist Protestant St. John's Chapel in Ruxton, still owned by members of the surviving Scott family.

A reunion of former Cross Keys Village residents include front row, left to right: *Geraldine Epps-Fowltes, Delores Johnson Johnson, June Hawkins Randall, Agnes Francine Crosby, Sharon McBride, Holly Harper.* Middle row: *Ed Chaney, Lelia Merritt Newkirk, Charles Seabreeze, Bernard McBride, Paul Johnson, Reita Bryant Carroll, Anthony Parker, John McBride, Delores Silva, Walter Gordon, Gertrude Harvey West.* Back row: *Lorenzo"Tony" Lee, Jesse Hawkins, Jerry Hynson, Ray Wheeler, Garland Crosby.*—James K. Lightner

Just before Rev. Scott's death, a dispute occurred among some of his parishioners that led to the formation of the second church in Cross Keys. The Scotts thought they were better than the rest of us, said a former parishioner. The new congregation first met in a nearby private home at 4647 Falls Road, then as membership increased, it was moved three houses south to 4641, which had been an early schoolhouse. In 1918, the church received acceptance into the AME Conference under Bishop Monroe Davis and Pastor Bev. O. Curtis and became known as the Falls Road AME. African Americans would come from Cross Keys, Bare Hills, Hoes Heights and other parts of Baltimore City for Sunday, holiday and special services at the two churches. Falls Road AME is now relocated in Woodlawn.

3

Villagers Remember

"We had a lot of fun in Cross Keys, or 'The Falls Road,' as we called it in my day," said 73-year-old Gertrude Harvey West whose early childhood was spent with five other siblings, Beatrice (Bunny), Delores (Lorsie), John (Bobby), Ardella (Dell) and Warren and her parents, Beatrice Lee and Llewellan (John) Harvey. Many children adopted nicknames given by younger siblings who couldn't pronounce their first names or their friends just started calling them the name because they thought it was better suited.

All the children played together in White Oak Grove and in the 'condu,' their name for the conduit storm drains that laced the nearby fields and emptied into Jones Falls. "Some of the boys said they could walk all the way into town inside the condu," said Gert. "In the meadow behind the school and portable class-rooms, we played softball, married women against singles and the men the same way, all different combinations. But us Harvey girls could beat anybody, even the men. Pop would always be the umpire. Oh, it was fun. I don't know how to describe Falls Road back then, but we participated in a lot of things. Our parents were interested in what we did. On Sundays after church we'd go to Miss Betty's Cafe, knock on the door and she or someone would open it a crack, see what we wanted, and bring us our soda and potato chips." Garland Crosby remembers those visits, too. "And we never got a choice," he said.

"Our first home at 4675 was on the east side of the road," said Gert West. "Downstairs there were the living and dining rooms and the kitchen. Upstairs were two bedrooms, one in the back for our parents and one up front that was partitioned—one side for boys and one side for girls. The toilet was out the kitchen door and around the corner. At night we'd all use the toilet *before* we went upstairs to bed, and for emergencies, we'd use a chamber pot filled with water and bleach. Us kids called it a slop pot. The oldest had to empty it in the morning."

Having lived at 4656 Falls Road, Jesse Hawkins, 75, regaled some of his former neighbors with the story about a group of noisy boys and girls congregating under a favorite streetlight. "It happened to be in front of a lady's house, for some reason, we used to call 'Taga Maude,' not to her face, but among us kids," he said. "I guess Mrs. Maude Hall got tired of the boisterousness and raised her upstairs' bedroom window. Now we knew she didn't have an inside bathroom, but were we surprised when she threw out a bucket of 'overnight.' It got all over us, in the girl's hair, down our fronts. What a mess! Remember that, Sally?" he asked.

"I sure do," said Sally Kutch, making a face as she patted the side of her hair. Sally had lived at 4686 Falls Road. She was a pretty young girl who sometimes would be taken advantage of by the other kids. Once when her grandfather, Charles Brown, was asleep in his chair and snoring, the older children gave her some moldy cheese and convinced her to try to toss a piece into her relaxed grandfather's open mouth. "They told me not to stop until I got a piece in," she said. After a number of tries, success! But the pelting woke up old Charles. Now in those days all the Brown men wore heavy pointed shoes and Sally "got a swift kick on her shin that really hurt to the bone," she grimaced. "I was stupid. I'd do anything they'd say. My grandmother found out about the kick and wouldn't speak to him for a week," said Sally.

"Our grandparents raised chickens in backyard coops," continued Gertrude West. "Some of my younger brothers and sisters didn't want to eat *our* chickens' eggs so my mother had to go to the store to buy a dozen eggs and mix them in with our eggs so we wouldn't know which were which. I guess all kids are strange sometimes. I remember my grandmother wringing a chicken's neck, then letting it go to run around the yard to die. I really didn't like that.

"There were many interesting things about life in the village," she said. "There were traditions, like Monday was for washing, Tuesday ironing, but stranger than that, on certain days of the week, *every* family in the village ate the same thing. As an example, every Thursday was cabbage day. *Everyone* had cabbage, stewed tomatoes, white potatoes and a meat. Friday was fish day for everyone; Saturday was bean soup. We'd buy a piece of fatback for fifteen cents and add the beans. On Sunday we had chicken. The other days were whatever each family wanted. You could smell those days for miles.

"And of course, Saturday evening, we all took baths. In the very early days of my childhood, we got our water from an outside well between 4771 and 73. But my uncle covered the well with a wooden platform when he saw that we had put up a swing on a nearby tree. Years later, the city ran water pipes to our house. Even though we only had cold water, it was a luxury when compared with carrying buckets of water from a well with a heavy cover over it. For our baths, mother would heat up the teakettle on the gas stove and fill a big tin tub in the kitchen. Then the door was closed and the oldest child got in first, washed and dried off while the kettle was heating up for the next. After we all finished, the two biggest children would grab the handles and take the tub out back to empty it.

"I started elementary school at 158 in a portable classroom," said Gert. "There were three portables for the first three grades and were located down the hill from the school. Grades four through six were in the main school right on Falls Road. It looked like one of the residences except it had a flagpole angled from the second floor. As the number of children declined, the portables were taken over by city agencies. The whole school closed in the mid-50s.

"From the time I was eleven, I worked," said Gert West. "I'd come home from school and go to the [Charles] Slagles at 4803 Roland Avenue. I was a cook at first. My grandmother cooked for the Slagles in the big house and my father and uncle were their chauffeurs. As I got older, I worked at 211 Ridgewood Road. I'd walk back Spatts Lane [the way "Spath" used to be spelled and pronounced], up the dirt path to the back of Ridgewood at the [W. Fairfield] Peterson's then on to my job. I also worked at Miss Taylor's rooming house that was at 508 Woodlawn Road. Then I would work for the Slagles only on Saturday. I worked for them until I was nineteen.

The earliest colored school in Cross Keys Village was on the east side of Falls Road. Here one of its classes poses in the side yard. When the new #158 was completed across the road, the old school became a meeting hall and later, the Falls Road AME Church. Tony Parker's uncle, Simon Casper Parker, is seen in the center of the back row with a white collar.—Tony and Holly Parker

"When I got married in 1952 we moved away, but in 1956 we returned to 4630 and indoor plumbing. Falls Road was one big family" She repeated it for emphasis, "It was really one big family—until word came that the city was going to buy up the houses in Cross Keys and tear them down to make room for the new expressway and schools. We were going to have to move. It was sad for a lot of people, particularly the elderly who could find displacement difficult to handle." Some residents thought the money was good, and like Jerry Hynson's parents, felt they were 'bettering themselves' by moving to Govans.

By then young Jerry was bettering himself. He worked at Hoffman's Market on Falls, just south of Coldspring. "Mr. Frank expected me to attend Morgan State and continue to work in his store," said Hynson. "But Judge Dulany Foster had a different idea. He wanted me to attend St. John's College, the classic book school in Annapolis. I had applied, but was still uncertain. Then one day just before I was to report to St. John's, I was loading Judge Foster's groceries into his car and he said firmly, 'Jerry, I don't expect you to be working here in two weeks.' I'm sure he had made the arrangements for my scholarship.

"I had always been interested in books," said Jerry. As a youngster, I'd go with Mom as she did domestic work for Eugene Williams in Roland Park. Mr. Williams was president of the Western Maryland Railway." said Hynson. "He had an extensive library and I would take down books and read them. Once he came home and saw me reading. It was an embarrassment for my mother, but he said 'Eunice, any book he wants, let him take it home to read.' I'll never forget that kindness."

Here are some of the few remaining homes on the east side of Falls Road in Cross Keys Village. See others on top of front cover. Most of the homes were torn down for a fast food strip mall, nursing center, pharmacy and service stations.

It was a heartrending experience for many of the Cross Keys residents when notice was given that they had to move. "There was no community meeting," said Gert West. "City Hall just gave us three options. The first offer for your house was one amount of money, the second was for some more, and if you thought your house was worth more, you had to go to court and sue. That was the third option and who could afford that?" she said waving her arms in the air signaling her frustration. "They didn't take the Falls Road homes until about 1960 or 61. By then I had a family. Fortunately we were living on the east side of Falls Road, up on the hill, and that side survived for a while.

Ed Chaney, 62, a former resident of the community and police officer, pointed out the underlying problem. "In those days, many black people just did what they were told. We had no power or political influence. Maybe someone wanted to clear us off of Falls Road. Today when you look at the empty parking lot of Western High which was the backyards of our west side homes, you have to ask why it was necessary to move us."

Billie Branhall, a national planning consultant, added some further insight: "Baltimore did some creative things downtown...but the planners were really ruthless in removing black families without adequate compensation. There were no relocation benefits," she said. "I was struck by the lack of equity in the urban renewal program." Some called the effort, "Negro removal."

Gert West and her husband had nine children, and she can rattle off their names and birth dates like a riveting gun. And I have forty-seven grand and great grandchildren," she adds. As she got older, Mrs. West worked as a crossing guard and teacher at Head Start. At the same time she was catering parties in Roland Park. "I got to meet some wonderful people," she said.

Ed Chaney was quick to remind Gert how *credit* was a problem for blacks in those days. "Even our refrigerator had a coin box on it," he said. "You had to put at least one quarter in everyday and every time you opened the door, another quarter. The same for your television. Many people are familiar with putting quarters in a washer or dryer, but your refrigerator? That's the way it used to be."

"I guess I was the kid on the block," said Michael Douglass, "but Gert West and I have remained friends. The 55-year-old Lochearn resident once lived at 4635 Falls Road, two doors from Miss Bettie's bar. "I was three or four when we moved there and I can remember attending Cub Scouts with Jerry Hynson's younger brother, Lemuel. Mike recalled the "Tom Thumb" mock weddings between the little girls and boys for church fundraisings. I played with the Gaskin children, although the twins were older than me. I can remember Tony Lee. He was the neighborhood bully," he laughed. As a youngster, Mike kept busy cutting grass and shoveling snow. In the late 1950s, he joined the U. S. Navy serving on the first nuclear aircraft carrier, *Enterprise*, as an expert in explosive ordnance disposal during the Vietnam War. He saw combat doing temporary duty on a riverboat. No, he can't handle war movies like "Apocalypse Now." "Too realistic," he confides.

After discharge, Mike attended the University of Maryland, moved to California, married and returned to Baltimore where he is vice president of DJ Management, an accounting firm. On the side, he is a fencing master and coaches the team at UMBC, traveling to competitions at colleges along the east coast. "When I got out of the Navy and came back to Falls Road, it was like a ghost town over there. Everything on the west side of the road was gone, leveled," he said. Mike is related to Frederick Douglass through Charles Douglass who served in the Union army in North Carolina. "He was my great, great uncle, I believe."

The mystery building in Cross Keys Village is the horse stable at 4721 Falls Road. It actually stands in Roland Park, but just barely. In the earliest days, it was a private stable for the Thomas S. Symington family who lived on Ridgewood Road. It was on the adjacent lot down hill. The late Luther S. Tall wrote in his memoirs that he "could remember Mr. Thomas Symington's tally-ho [four-in-hand coach] coming down Roland Avenue and turning over Wynhurst Road to the Elkridge Hunt Club on Charles Street. The hounds would run along with the horses. In those days it was legal to keep horses and carriages, if there was a rear lane." Roland Park had its own apartment stables in back of the commercial properties at Roland Avenue and Upton Road as did the Baltimore Country Club and eight private residents.

The mystery building of Falls Road, the 100-year-old Symington horse stable, is now renovated into a showplace residence. It is located on Falls Road behind a screen of hemlocks at the very edge of Roland Park, next to Cross Keys Village.

The one-time Symington stable is now the home of Gerald and Ann Walsh. They have been as intrigued by their unique home as anyone would be who has spotted its spire and cupola over the growth of hemlocks on Falls Road, just south of Hillside. Recently, they have converted its stalls and hay chutes into a showplace. "We removed everything but the floor," said Ann. "One of the hardest jobs was rewiring the electric because we had to drill into the old timbers which had petrified." Over the century, the building had served many purposes. "It had once been an antique store with a number of employees," she said.

Before the Walshes, for thirty-five years Bill and Mary Lee Temmink lived in the dwelling. "We moved into the building in 1948," said Bill. "The former owner, Floyd Peyton, had used the southend of the house, the stable end, as a furniture upholstery shop. We came from Catonsville to look for something larger for our six children," said Temmink, now a Ruxton resident. Explaining the floor plan, he said you entered through the kitchen although there was a front door that came into a small room, separated from the kitchen by a wall. "The north end was nothing more than a large garage with five large doors for horses and carriages to pass," he said. "To get to the rooms above what became a living room, you had to climb a ladder and go through a trapdoor. There was no connection between that upper room and the adjacent bedrooms. When we broke through the walls, we found an eight-inch difference in the height of the floors.

"The building is constructed of concrete blocks twelve inches high and wide and thirty inches long," said Temmink. "We had to cut some down to put in windows and found, between every two layers, steel beams a half-inch thick by four inches wide by ten feet long. They were brutes to work with. Each block was marked with the name and address of a New York manufacturer. Can you imagine having them shipped that distance to Baltimore?" Most people believe the stable was constructed around the turn of the century, about the time the Symington house was built. "They had horses and grooms living in the stable building," he said.

Two decades have passed since the Temminks lived in the stable. "Right at the outset, my father and I planted all those hemlocks along Falls Road when they were only four feet high. Look at them now. We also put in a fireplace and added an apartment for my mother-in-law." Temmink remembers Hurricane Agnes in 1972 and the rampaging stream near the Roland Park tennis facility that stormed over Falls Road and created a fifteen-acre lake on the Poly-Western athletic field. "It was a great sight," he said.

As the present owners, the Walshes have made many more changes to the home with gardens and patios, bay window and new interior layout and decor. It can now be considered a show place for Roland Park, a mansion with an interesting lineage.

Top, *Vertelle Hall was instrumental in setting up a reunion of former residents of Cross Keys Village. This led to the interviews for this book.* Bottom, *Paul Johnson created a map of families living in Cross Keys Village in the 1930s to present. (See Appendix.) He stands in front of 4703 and 4705 Falls Road, homes that may be demolished for commercial buildings.*

Paul Johnson, a retired school principal, took a sentimental walk along his former Cross Keys Village neighborhood starting just across from the stable property. "You can still get the feeling of the old place," he said as he strolled south along the west side of Falls Road. "Over there in that space between the vacant lot and the north end of ManorCare is where Oakdale Road used to be. We lived up there at 1105 on the right side of Oakdale, in one of the two duplexes, four dwellings, going all the way back to that stone wall. The wall was sort of a backdrop where we took many of our holiday and celebration pictures. I remember burying my box of childhood paper-dolls right there at the wall. It was the end of a passage in my life. I can't believe how high and steep it is back there. When I was a child, the land seemed to slope gently to the road. The Tyson Church was over on the corner. On this side of the Falls Road [west] were homes that were built below grade. I guess some of them had three to five steps to get down to the front porch. That's another thing about Cross Keys Village. We all had porches and people sat on them, talked with their neighbors, even waved to the trolley conductors.

"It's a little hard to visualize now that the high schools are so prominent in the background, but in the old days there was a yellow-green pasture over there," he said looking toward the Jones Falls. "There were cows grazing and a stream flowing through it. I'm told the farm was run until 1910 by a local guy named Davis Baker who had a dairy at the southern end of the village and sold the milk to homes and stores and, I suppose, folks could buy some of it at Mr. Douglass's store over there," he said pointing to the only brick building now standing, just south of ManorCare. "He and Mrs. Douglass lived on the second floor. I understand that Mr. Baker was a prominent citizen and had a residence fronting on Coldspring Lane, and his stables and outbuildings were scattered on the slope behind.

"The entrance road on the right of the health care center is about where Spath Lane ran back from the main road with three or four houses on each side. It just occurred to me that pieces of broken macadam pavement still shows where Oakland Road was on the left of ManorCare. There were three trolley stops in the early days of the village. I think we ended up with one bus stop opposite the midway point of the ManorCare building. Simon Scott's big house would have been located in the middle of the existing building. Fifty feet south of ManorCare once stood the Falls Road AME Church, just north of the Douglass store."

*ManorCare nursing center stands between what used to be Oakdale Road
and Spath Lane. Simon Scott's salvage yard would have been in the rear
center of the building with a trolley stop in front center.*

As he walked along, Johnson's attention was drawn to a group of high school children drinking sodas on a steps leading to the CVS Pharmacy. To their left was an overgrown lot where Scotty's (Miss Bettie's) Cafe once stood. "They're a little older than we were, but kids are still kids. The youth of today have a lot more money than we did, but I doubt that they are any happier. Our school, Number 158, was a clapboard building on this side of the road just about halfway between Hillside and the corner at Coldspring." Its facade was flush with those of the homes. Just south of the portable classrooms in back of the school was an open field where we used to play ball." For a moment he stopped, looking toward the sun setting across the Western High School parking lot. "Right here [across from CVS] was the old Cross Keys Inn," he said, pointing at the grassy strip that rolled down to the asphalt. Of course I don't remember the Cross Keys tavern, but I can still see the big house that sat on the same foundation after the inn burned in 1909."

Left, *Charles Lynch rides his pedal car behind two duplexes on Oakdale Road. In the background are homes in Roland Park.* Center, *Ann Lee Johnson, left, and her sister-in-law, Vivian Brown Lee, in front of the "ceremonial wall" that still can be seen at the left of ManorCare on Falls Road. Vivian married Ann's youngest brother, William Lee.* Right, *Paul and Mary Johnson with their mother (Ann Lee Johnson) and their father Edgar's car.*—Paul Johnson

Facing the brown and cream brick high school, Johnson said the land first sloped down from the backs of the homes on the west side. "There was an open lot and stream down there before the city made it a dump. It was like a landfill, but then people threw garbage in it so there was an odor during the summer. On the other side of the dump, the land rose up a hill covered by woods with the Jones Falls behind them.

"Most everyone had an outhouse in the early days or a shed of some kind at the back end of the lot that was used for lawn equipment, storage or junk," he said. "Speaking of junk, over there behind most of ManorCare once stood Simon Scott, Jr.'s salvage yard. There were all kinds of derelict cars, buses, motors and parts. He collected everything, even glass bottles. He'd drive his truck loaded with junk up Oakdale, then cut across the back to his property and sort out the pieces. Shielded by all the houses including his own, you couldn't see the junk-yard from Falls Road. When World War II came, he made a lot of money, bought up a lot of property around here and in other parts of Baltimore. He died a wealthy man April 1, 1961."

CVS Pharmacy is located across the road from where the 200-year-old Cross Keys Inn was located before it burned to the ground in the winter of 1909. The empty lot to the left was once the site of Scott's Beer Garden.

Turning again to face across the road, he smiled and said, "That was White Oak Grove, once the play field for children and adults for the best part of the nineteenth century." Now the former picnic ground is a CVS pharmacy and a locked-in maze of buildings, strip mall and alleyways under the "Golden Arches." Not a hint of its earlier pleasures. When Paul Johnson arrived at the corner of Falls and Coldspring, he just stood there. He was silent. Then he shook his head. "We had a great life here," he said. "Cross Keys Village was good to all of us."

Over the years romance bloomed in Cross Keys Village with so many children and so many of the same age, it was expected that old chums would get married. Some did, but not all. Ernestine Palmer, 84, remembers being on the trolley coming across the rickety Keswick bridge to Falls Road. "I had a boyfriend, Oscar Porter, who lived on Dewey Avenue in nearby Hoes Heights. I always wished the trolley would break down coming across the bridge so I could be with him longer," she said. "I was crazy about him.

"I only lived in Cross Keys for five years, came in 1938," said Ernestine, "and I still remember the fun we had on summer nights taking a grill to the woods up on the country club property to cook hot dogs and marshmallows. My father worked for George N. Brown's nephew who put music machines [juke boxes] in nightclubs as entertainment. And I think that's how we could afford our house on Falls Road. We always imagined that the folks on the west side of the road were better off than the other side…with the exception of Mr. Simon Scott, Jr., of course," she said.

Ben Mason, another former resident, is a well-connected, successful business-man. As a child, he lived downtown on Robert Street, but his folks feared for him crossing two major thoroughfares to attend first and second grade, so they'd bring him out to school 158 in Cross Keys where his uncle George N. Brown worked as custodian and could look after him. "I remember those Falls Road days very well," he said. "I was probably five or six when I fell in love with Colleen Gaskins. She had the most beautiful gray-green eyes. And remember those 'Tom Thumb' weddings? We did have fun.

"As I got older I'd go to the silent movies at the Scott's Church. I still recall 'Birth of a Nation.' And, how we'd gather around the radio and listen to Batman, Lone Ranger and The Shadow. Of course we all enjoyed going to Mr. Douglass's store. Because we never had our own telephone, if anyone would ask us for *our* number, we always replied 467-5286. That was the store's," said Mason.

Garland Crosby knew the old grocer as did everyone in the community. "Someone might call the store and tell Mr. Douglass they'd like to talk with so-and-so," he said. "Mr. Douglass would put the handset aside, go out in front and yell the caller's name. The word would be relayed up and down the block until so-and-so came to the store to get the call."

Perhaps Bernard McBride knew the Douglasses best of all. "I lived at 4662 and used to work at the store after school and on Saturdays. I went with Mr. Douglas to pick up the produce, I stocked shelves, cleaned chickens and made deliveries. And on Sundays, they took me downtown to Trinity Baptist Church at Druid Hill Avenue and McMechen Street. When we got back we had dinner and after we finished, I was allowed to go downstairs to the store and pick out any dessert I wanted, which was usually a pint of ice cream. They were nice peo-ple.

"Sometimes I'd split wood for stoves," said Bernard. "One time "Doc" White asked me to cut some for him. He'd been drinking and after it was getting dark, he asked me how many bushels I'd split and I told him five more than I had done. He said 'How could you have done that many, you haven't been at it that long?' So when I told him the truth, he said, 'That's about right.'"

Delores Johnson got religion early in her life. "I lived at 4671 and on Sundays went to church in Mt. Washington with my grandmother who was Methodist and later in the day I went with her brother to Pimlico. He was Baptist. So I was a Methodist-Baptist until I got older and joined the AME on Falls Road. My grandmother was a religious woman. She was always holding prayer meetings at home. My mother, as a young girl, was very rebellious and while all that praying and singing was going on, she and Dorothy Wilson would be up and down Falls Road raising Cain.

"Often my grandmother would send me to the store," recalled Delores. "But I had a habit of forgetting. This one time she said, 'Now don't forget. I want you to get a loaf of bread.' So I'd go skipping to Mr. Douglass's store singing, loaf of bread, loaf of bread, loaf of bread. And when I went inside and they asked me what I wanted, I said a quart of milk."

There were a lot of sports played in the village, baseball and softball, mainly. According to Walter Gordon, formerly of 4675 Falls Road, his grandson played soccer on the Olympic team and he remembers the days when neighbors' Buck and Jun Webster played semi-pro baseball with the "Falls Road Invincibles." The team played in a clearing overlooking Northern Parkway.

Maybe it was shooting marbles that was most popular around the dusty back lots in Cross Keys. George N. Brown was the champion shooter and he used to invite everyone, especially the youngsters, to try to beat him. Ed Chaney said *he* was good, but old George was even better. They'd scribe a six-foot circle in the dirt using a couple of nails on a string. The game is sort of played like pool, but with two or more persons. Players had their favorite marbles that were their shooters. They may have been bigger and heavier or more colorfully swirled in glass than "pot" marbles. Each person would put an equal number of marbles in the center of the ring.

Baseball was a favorite pastime in Cross Keys Village. At times teams would get together on Sunday, up and down Falls Road. Shown are the Hollins Athletic Club "Rangers," a semi-professional team from the Bare Hills area. Front row, left to right: *Alphonso Cooper, Walter Scott, Charley Jones, Alex Brown;* Middle row: *Bud Wick, Tom Taylor, Ike Johnson, Ernest Bannon, Quill Scott, Simon Jones;* Back row: *Dick Scott, Clarence Scott.* —Marie Scott Brown

To find out the order of shooting, a line was drawn in the dirt and each person would shoot to see who gets closest to the line. Then the first shooter aimed at the pot and tried to knock one or more marbles from the ring. If no marble gets hit hard enough to leave the ring, the next shooter had his turn. Eventually all the shooters were inside the circle near the pot and it became easier to knock out another marble. You kept shooting if you knocked one out and you got to keep those you knocked out of the circle. The "winner" was the person who went home with the most marbles. Vertelle Hall could shoot with the best of the boys. "Sometimes I'd tell them, no 'knuks' in the games I played," she said. Knuckle shooters shot a super-fast marble off their thumb knuckle and fore finger, so fast that it could shatter the glass marbles it struck. "See you fellas [and Vertelle] tomorrow," was George Brown's usual comment at the end of the games.

Top left, clockwise: *Sam Brown in front of his Falls Road home. Sam married Marie Scott after a courtship that saw them acclaimed "the best ballroom dancers in the area."*
Paul Johnson's maternal grandmother, Mary Ellen Taylor Lee, at the rear of her home at 1105 Oakdale Road in Cross Keys Village.
Leroy Lynch hugged by his sister Mildred with 4703 Falls Road in the background. Leroy lived at 1107 Oakdale Road in Cross Keys Village.—Paul Johnson

4

Upcountry, the Chapel and Marie

Anna Marie Julius Scott Brown, a direct descendant of the Scott patriarch, Tobias, and the last of her generation, was a stunning, well-mannered and popular young woman becoming prominent in black society. She lived north at "the other end" of Falls Road in Bare Hills, Baltimore County's old chrome and copper mining district. In colonial times, travelers to Bare Hills reported "barren hills" of rocky "white clay" soil, an absence of tall trees that were needed to build houses and fences, and "nothing to eat but berries."

Marie's father and mother were William Walter and Henrietta Scott, whom she called Pop and Mom, but with strangers, she referred to them as Papa and Mama. Her parents had four boys and four girls: Lewis, Ethel, Walter, Esther, Roberta, Marie and Harry, the youngest. A baby Howard died at birth. "We lived at 6234 Falls Road in a nice comfortable house," Marie said. "We kept a cow, pigs, chickens and horses. Once we had a calf, but she broke her leg while grazing across the road at the school so we had to kill her. We loved to collect mushrooms up on the hill when they popped out of the ground. And there were blackheart cherry and sickle pear trees near the cemetery.

"In the winter, if the family ran short of coal," recalled Marie, "some of us would go down to the railroad tracks at Hollins Station [earlier called Relay House, and later Bare Hills Station and Greenspring Junction] near Lake Roland and wait for a train. We used to think the engineer could make the train shake out some coal, but now I think it was the fireman shoveling it out to us. We'd pick up the chunks in a canvas bag and drag it home.

When it snowed," said Marie, "we'd all go sleigh riding on Falls Road from Walnut Avenue down to the bridge across Jones Falls or we'd go up to the Tracy place, a white family, and go down the hills in back of our houses. As I recall, Mr.

Tracy worked for the railroad. I think the Pennsylvania. His son, Bud, was always at our home. There has never been a problem with integration in Bare Hills"

Local "Pennsy" Railroad train, southbound at Hollins Station, c. 1930. At left is Greenspring branch of the railroad heading west.—R. K. Henry

Because of segregation laws, young Marie could not attend Bare Hills School, which was directly across Falls Road from where she lived. Rather, she and five of her brothers and sisters had to "walk the railroad tracks two-and-a-half miles" to the "colored" school at the end of Kelly Avenue in Mt. Washington. It was run by a wealthy African American teacher, Louise [E. G.] Derricks, who had moved from Long Green Valley. First she built the church, then her big frame house and a row of single frame homes east of the church. Derricks taught in the church building until a school could be built on the other side of Kelly Avenue. Marie added: "Sometimes the white children in Mt. Washington would try to pick a fight with us as we headed for school or home, but we survived."

Bare Hills School was built to educate children of local white mine workers.

Bare Hills School across the road from Marie's home was built in 1881 with the pale-green native serpentine stone for which Bare Hills is noted. It was a two-room structure for the white children of workers who mined ore in the area. It still stands today. It is the oldest public school in continuous use in Baltimore County. Students had to be cautioned about falling into the dangerous mine shafts nearby, which tunneled as far south as Mt. Washington. Marie once went into the entrance of one tunnel, but she said, her brothers "Walter, Harry and Lewis used to go way back inside the mine off Pimlico Road. They said the walls were green and there were a lot of lizards down there."

Left, *The church parsonage had been a tenant farmhouse, c. 1799.* Right,
*St. John's African Methodist Episcopal Chapel was built in 1886. An earlier
log church was destroyed by fire.*

Her first family church was St. John's in Ruxton. Early on, residents of the
enclave called it the "Bare Hills church" even though it was in Ruxton. As a
youngster Marie walked along a well-worn path around Lake Roland to St.
John's. It was about a mile east of her home and she carried a lantern for the
return trip at night. Some churchgoers rode the train from Hollins Station to
Lake Station near the church. The railroad reduced train schedules in later years
after the automobile became popular, and Marie would join the family in the
back of her brother-in-law John Gardman's pickup truck for an exciting ride
across the valley to church. "It was particularly exciting if Walter was driving,"
she said. When the weather was bad in winter, Marie held Sunday school in her
home.

"I loved the singing at St. John's," said Marie. "Colored singing has more life
in it, I've been told, and I believe it." As young women, Marie, Helen Richardson
and Carolyn Hall would ride the train to Lutherville for piano lessons from Ethel
Cummings, a minister. After they became proficient, they'd take turns playing
the pump organ at St. John's.

"Many colored people in Ruxton were from the South and they always came
to church," she said. "Ruxton was a place you could count on. The white folks
didn't think of us as help. They took care of us and our children like we were
family. The black church has always been a place for social entertainment, singing and hearing the word of God. It was one of the few places we could get
together and enjoy each other. On Wednesday evenings after eight, we'd get
together for a literary in the church. Parishioners from Bare Hills would debate

those from Ruxton. One would have to defend an interpretation of biblical text. Then the audience would participate. Now that I think of it, church was mostly a nighttime activity. Even on Sunday, after live-ins had served the main meal around two o'clock, by the time things were cleaned up and they were dressed, it was early evening."

In the 1950s St. John's started losing congregants. "Folks were dying out and there were fewer live-in help to come to services." explained Marie. "By then the trains had mostly stopped. By 1960, the trustees decided it was time to close the chapel. Colored folks continued to meet in the railroad station hanging out until the 8:45 train arrived, one of the few still running (compared with thirty-five that ran each day in 1892). During those years after closing, we still held a few special services at St. John's when Rev. Blackledge, Rev. Davis or another minister would visit. We couldn't afford to pay them because we lost our tax-exemtion except for the cemetery. Oh there were white folk who supported the church by coming to the services and helping in so many ways. Some of them are buried in St. John's cemetery, right along side my Mom and Pop."

With the closing of St. John's, Marie sometimes went to church in Stevenson, but most often she attended Tyson Church in Cross Keys Village near where many of her cousins lived. To get there she would walk from her Bare Hills home to Mount Washington and take the No. 25 trolley to the church near Cold Spring Lane. "Falls Road was something in those days," she said.

Graduating from Douglass High School, Marie was an athletic youngster. She played tennis and volleyball at Druid Hill with Carl Douglass (son of Parker) and her sister Roberta, but with all her athletic prowess, Marie never learned to swim. "Once," she said, "I saw a drowned man brought to shore at Lake Roland. It wasn't a pretty sight and after that I was afraid to try." She also remembers the tragic drowning of Josephine Fenwick's sister who fell out of a canoe into the lake on her sixteenth birthday. Mrs. Fenwick had lived in the Bare Hills enclave and was the midwife who delivered Marie. She also recalled that her cousin Julius's brother, George, drowned while serving as a chauffeur for the Goodwillys of Guilford who were summering in New Hampshire.

Marie Scott Brown, 92, inscribes a family Bible given to her for St. John's Chapel by the Shacklefords of Roland Park.

Marie worked for several "Blue Book" families in Roland Park including the furniture people, the [William B.] Fallons at 6 Elmhurst Road. She also catered parties for the TeLindes, Helfriches, Symingtons, Edmundses, Freitags and Shackelfords, to name a few. Proudly she refers to the big family Bible Mrs. Shackelford gave her for use at St. John's after her husband passed away. Originally the Bible was inscribed by the Shackelfords on January 9, 1841. After the Bible was recently re-bound in leather, Mrs. Brown wrote in it: Given to St. John's Church by Dr. Schalford [sic] April 28, 2002. Anna Marie Brown.

"Josey Boy" Addison was chauffeur for three Baltimore mayors, shown here with a son of Mayor Jackson. The resident of Bare Hills was allowed to drive his children to and from school and kept the car in a special garage built onto his home.—Marie Scott Brown

Marie's brother-in-law, Joe "Josey Boy" Addison, was chauffeur for three Baltimore mayors beginning with William Broening, then Howard Jackson and finally, Theodore McKeldin. As part of his daily run, Joe was allowed to pick up some of the Bare Hills children and take them to and from school. At night, he'd park the mayor's car in a double garage at his home at 6203 Falls Road.

Marie Scott and three sisters, Roberta, Ethel and Esther, also worked as maids for thirty-five years at the Lyric Theater in downtown Baltimore. "Mayor Broening had arranged for Ethel to get a job at the Lyric," said Marie. "She was the first. We wore black dresses and caps and were always neat. People always treated us kindly there. You never felt you were colored." It was in box seats at the Lyric where Marie got to know Rosa Ponselle, the great American soprano. "She was so nice." Because of Joe Addison's chauffeuring duties for Ponselle's brother-in-law, Mayor Jackson, Marie was often asked to cater parties at the Villa Pace estate in Greenspring Valley. "I'd stay up all night and fix everything right here in the kitchen," she said. "The whole family would help. Sometimes we even did two parties in one day," she said.

After luncheon on Thursday, "the maids night out," Marie would leave her job in Roland Park and take the trolley downtown and walk around window-shopping. "Then I'd come back to the Royal Theater to watch a movie and a show. "Remember how the lights would come up after the movie and the orchestra started playing and the stage show would start? Wonderful!" she exclaimed.

Marie would travel extensively in the summer. Sometimes she vacationed in Atlantic City, but most often her visits were with people who employed her. "Once I took the entire summer off," she laughed, "and went to work for a family in Rehoboth, Delaware. Another time I worked the summer in Lake Placid, right out on the lake. Oh, it was beautiful. And it snowed before we left at the end of the season."

Marie's passion was dancing, particularly after the Methodist Church dropped its ban on dancing and theatergoing in 1924. Her Catholic mother, Henrietta, and her friend Arizona Jenkins, taught her all the steps popular at the time. "When friends came over to the house, Miss Jenkins would bring her Victrola with a horn on top and we'd push back the table and chairs in the dining room and dance." After Marie separated from her first husband, Robert Walton, she went to formal dances every Friday night, often to the Wonder Pinochle Club at the Odd Fellow Hall on McCulloh Street. "One tried to outdo the other," she said. Her eyes sparkled as a friend commented on a photograph from her youth. "DeeDee [Marie's nickname, as is "Weesie"], you must have been a high stepper in that coat with the fur collar."

At one of the dances she met Sam Brown. "He was a very good dancer—oh lord, yes—we did lots of clubs then," said Marie. "We danced at the social hall in the bottom at St. John's. And there was a dance floor up in Hoes Heights, Hoes Hill as we called it, near Dewey Avenue. It was outside, no pavilion, just a big floor under the night sky. They had orchestras in the summer and no one complained about the noise. We also went to dances in the city and in Greenspring Valley. Sam was a wonderful dresser, particularly when we went formal. Once when we came home from a dance, there had been an accident in front of his house. Had it not been that the driver had hit a telegraph pole first, he'd have driven right into Sam's living room. When the man saw us in our formal clothes, he said 'Where'd you come from?' I guess he thought we could have been angels. Sam was a chef at the Marine Hospital," she said, "and there were lots of girls from there who came to the dances. I'd get beautiful gowns from the Hopkins Carry-on-Shop and we'd go! Waltzes were my favorite. My brother Lewis enjoyed waltzing too. In later years, to learn new ballroom steps, Sam and I would watch the Arthur Murray dance show on television. We were considered the best dancers wherever we went."

In the late 1930s, Marie and Sam were married. He lived in Cross Keys Village and was a charter member of Falls Road AME so she changed her affiliation from the Tyson Church. They never lived together in the village, but moved into the Scott home at 6203 Falls Road in Bare Hills. They had been married nearly twenty years when Sam's diabetes caused him to be hospitalized. He died of kidney failure November 13, 1961.

Marie also learned to cook from her mother who always had to have a lot of food in the house, especially for the baseball teams that would stop by after a Sunday game. "They'd eat everything in the house and there'd never be anything for our school lunches the next day," she said. "Sometimes relatives from the city would come out to visit and watch baseball. Papa often drove his carriage into Mt. Washington and meet them to make it easier for the older folks," she said. Later in life, Marie and other members of the family started a catering business employing several generations of siblings and cousins. "The Scotts made your party," said one elderly white Roland Park matron. "Unless the Scott girls were preparing the food or serving in their pretty toile aprons and caps, you just weren't at the top your game," she said.

Lewis Scott, Marie's brother, was a chauffeur for the Arthur and Rachel Hawks family in Ruxton. He is remembered by John Hawks, a grandson, as a strong gentle man who was always working: "He must have put in 27 hours a day, from our grandparents place, to Graul's Market and on to the L'Hirondelle Club." Marie also worked for the family and to this day John is impressed with her delicious turkey Tetrazzini. Marie was an admirer of Mrs. Hawks, by then a nationally known sculptor, whose stone eagles still lurk atop the corners of the old Chesapeake Cadillac building on Charles Street at 24th Street. A piece of Rachel Hawks' garden sculpture recently sold at auction for $8,000.

Mrs. Amy Brown Davis, in her 101st year, stands as she's recognized during services at the historic St. John's Chapel in Ruxton. She is wearing one of her feathered "church hats." Mrs. Davis is the wife of late Rev. George Davis, a former pastor of St. John's.

Proud of her heritage, Marie tells about some of the other close-knit African American communities around north Baltimore, all of which are still extant in Lutherville, Sparks, Shawan, Stevenson, East Towson, Cross Keys, Cockeysville, Ruxton as well as Bare Hills. "I still see friends and relatives from these areas," she said. "One of my dearest friends is Miss Amy Davis who has lived in East Towson for over fifty years. She's in her one hundred and first year, always happy, and still going strong. Her late husband George, who died in 1988, was pastor of St. John's for about five years." Amy, wearing one of her special church hats, still attends most of St. John's five annual services required to maintain its non-profit status. As a young girl living between Ward and Ridge Spring in South Carolina, Amy recalls how she'd clean flatware with ashes from the fireplace, polish the glasses with lard, settle her stomach with dry toast and warm water and cure a cough from a cold with onions around the neck and taking a spoonful of sugar and baking soda. Another of her home remedies: Banana peels soaked overnight in a jar of vinegar and patted on arthritic joints. To celebrate Amy's 100th birthday in September 2002, over five hundred persons attended two galas put on by her children.

In 2002 there were eighteen homes of African American (mostly Scott) families in the Bare Hills Historic District, many on Falls Road.

Marie Scott Brown's birth home still stands in Bare Hills as do seventeen other frame dwellings in what has become known as the Scott Settlement Historical District. Unfortunately Mathew Yates' home (c. 1848–1868, No.3 in the Scott Settlement map in the Appendix) was severely damaged by fire in December 2002. In the early days, the homes had outhouses and hand-dug wells. One stone and stucco two-story on the east side of Falls Road, owned by Alonzo and Nannie Yates (they also owned the Yates' house mentioned above on the west side as well as another) was torn down to make room for the Princeton Sports parking lot. Sarah Fenno Lord, a writer and preservationist, together with Susan E. Cook and Marie Fisher Cooke, among others, have made it their mission to preserve what is left of a most distinctive enclave of free blacks in Maryland and rare in the United States. For years the women have fought disinterest, harassment, developers and even a proposed I-83 interchange at Bare Hills.

The stone and stucco home on the left side of Falls Road was owned by Alonzo and Nannie Yates. It was torn down to make room for the Princeton Sports parking lot. In the background of this 1942 photograph is the Bare Hills School.—Baltimore County Library

Tobias, a young slave, was Marie Scott Brown's great grandfather. Believed to have been enslaved in the coastal jungles of Africa, Tobias is said to have been a field hand in St. Mary's County, Maryland, but Marie recently said, "He lived on the Eastern Shore as a slave" possibly on a tobacco plantation. At one time there were 25,000 slaves on the tidewater peninsula. Because tobacco took special care and could only be grown on the same land for three or four seasons, the crop was probably losing its profitability in Maryland except for the southern-most counties. When tobacco lost its value, slaves became an expensive liability for plantation owners. Perhaps Tobias's master sold him to a slave ship captain.

It was in the late 1700s, sometime after the American Revolution, that young Tobias earned his freedom when, according to oral family history, he saved the life of his captain and others aboard a slave ship that had sailed from America (possibly out of Oxford or Annapolis, important Maryland ports in those days). It was bound for England with a cargo such as indigo, cotton or tobacco, then on to West Africa where it would stop at one of the slave-holding compounds constructed by European slavers along three hundred miles of west Africa coastline. Carolyn Scott LeVere, a great great granddaughter, thinks that Tobias may have been used to communicate with captured slaves, may have even tried to comfort them about their future in America.

Once loaded, the ship would beat back across the Atlantic to Maryland where its surviving human cargo would be sold at auction. Depending on ship size, traders would bring as few as six slaves or as many as two hundred.

Holly Parker, a history and anthropology student in college, recently put forward the theory that Tobias may have been educated by his African forebears on the healing powers of certain roots and herbs. When the captain and crew of the slaver fell ill from typhus, known as ship's fever, or perhaps some other disease prevalent among sailors, Tobias was able to mix up a life-saving African concoction.

Manumitted, Tobias may have been given a surname especially if he was to get a freedom pass. In any event, he ended up with the last name of Scott. Author Ralph Clayton who has done extensive research on slaves in Maryland says less then twenty-five percent of the slaves were named after their owners. Quite often they took the surnames of famous persons, admired friends or relatives.

Some of the dates of Tobias's birth and migration are still debated. There is no record of him in the census, but that could have been due to errors in census taking or even a plantation master hiding his "property" to lower his taxes.

There is speculation that American Indians, once living in the Bare Hills section of Baltimore County, were run off by colonists in the mid-1700s and a few resettled in St. Mary's County. Blacks, Indians and whites often co-mingled and became known locally (to this day) as "Wesorts." Because the Scotts share the same inter-racial mixture and have Southern Maryland ties, it is possible that Scott family ancestors were Wesorts. There is miscegenation in Charles County, some in St. Mary's County and in Delaware around Wilmington. According to Ruth Hill, who works in the archives of the Leonardtown Historical Society, the name Wesort, or "Wesaw" as it is pronounced locally, sprang from "We sort of people," a phrase which sort of implies they are a race unto themselves. She also noted Wesorts in Charles County are often referred to as STPs which stands for the predominant family names of Savoy, Swann, Thompson and Proctor. According to Greg Coates, a descendent in Charles County, the term STP is a derogatory term for the racially blended people and is seldom used today. One of the Wesorts may have been Tobias's mother.

From the marriage of Tobias and his wife (name unknown), records show only one child, James Aquilla Scott, born in 1784. In later life, Aquilla never used his first name. There is a record of a minister, Aquilla Scott, who baptized children in Harford County and that could help substantiate Marie Scott Brown's recent recollection that Tobias had lived as a slave on the Eastern Shore. It is a long, but relatively easy walk from the Shore up and around the headwaters of the

Chesapeake through Cecil County to Harford County. Or, it is possible that Marie, like many Marylanders, thinks of St. Mary's County as the "Eastern Shore."

Rev. James Aquilla Scott, Sr., master blacksmith and first minister of St. John's when it was a log church, died of a heart attack in 1858 while delivering a sermon.—Marie Scott Brown

Whatever the circumstances, Aquilla Scott had migrated north to Bare Hills in the early 1830s and stayed in quarters with friends. Soon he met and married Priscilla and they had twelve children: John, William, Johanna, James, Mary, Ellen, James Aquilla, Jr., Priscilla, Susana, George, Nathaniel and Edward. Aquilla Scott became the area's first smithy and wheelwright at a time when the aging and poorly maintained surface of the Falls Turnpike Road was taking its toll on wagon wheels and horseshoes.

Apparently Aquilla was able to convince the owner of the land in Bare Hills to allow him to build a house for his growing family. A skilled blacksmith, Aquilla was also a man of God. He cleared the land of briars and dwarf pine trees and built his first church, a small log structure, only a few hundred feet to the rear of his home, according to Caroline Scott LeVere.

Rev. Aquilla Scott built several homes for his extended family. "A. Scott" and "Yates" homes are shown on the 1850 map by J. C. Sidney & P. J. Browne. Some of the Bare Hills dwellings now have been occupied by six generations of Scotts. Aquilla wanted it that way and told his children that the land was preserved for blacks, preferably Scotts, who couldn't find a suitable lot or home in the city. Most descendants have made the same provision. When a white family bought one of the homes recently, Sarah Fenno Lord, herself white, said, "There goes the neighborhood."

Oral history says this line of Scotts were all free-born in the Bare Hills area and, from the earliest days, were able to read and write, earn wages, own businesses, and acquire tracts of land and homes. But during those years of American history, no blacks—free or slave—were allowed to vote or hold office, and were subject to other injustices. The same was true of Catholics and Jews. However, it is interesting to note that in 1787, after the Revolutionary War, egalitarian Maryland was one of three states that *did* extend these rights to blacks and others for a short period. It must have encouraged Thomas Brown, a free-black horse doctor, to run for the Maryland legislature in 1792, although his tally was too small to have been recorded.

The next year the Fugitive Slave Law was passed, calling for the return of any runaway slave. The cotton gin was invented in the same year (1793) making it easier and faster to clean the raw cotton, thus requiring more slaves to cultivate the crop. With hope for freedom dwindling, more and more young male slaves made plans to escape their bondage. The "underground railroad," sometimes referred to as "The Gospel Train" picked up speed as the new century got under way.

The white political system was struggling to come up with solutions for the "African American issue." After 1796, rights of Maryland free blacks declined as their numbers increased and with the 1802 amendment, they were again denied the vote. To simplify many proposed ideas, "sweeping racial generalizations were necessary." Free blacks and slaves had to be put in the same lesser category," said an American history lecturer at Oxford University. "This coherent racist doctrine...became a sacred, significant totem in American society," he said. From the mid-1800s to 1864, even southern white churches gave their special imprimatur to slavery. Church separatism was sectional politics by another name. In the South, Baptists, Methodists and Presbyterians were pro-slavery avowed to "conserve the institution of slavery and to make it a blessing both to master and slave."

It was in the early 1800s that Federalist Robert Goodloe Harper and others were organizing a movement to return all blacks—slave and free—back to Africa.

In 1832, construction of the Baltimore & Susquehanna Railroad from Baltimore City continued through Ruxton and cut off the northeast three-quarter acre corner of the original *Hector's Hopyard* tract from the remaining 16 acres then owned by the Elijah Fishpaw family. On October 28, 1833, the Fishpaws sold the virtually useless land in Ruxton for "$15 to several freed slaves" including Aquilla Scott. In the deed, their organization is referred to as the "Bethel Episcopal Methodist Religious Society."

Found in the Towson courthouse is this copy of the 1833 agreement between the Fishpaw family and the trustees who bought the land for a log church in which to worship.

Under the agreement, the land had to be used to erect a church and burying ground (a cemetery had long been established there) or revert to the former owners or heirs. The Deed of Transfer granted the rectangular three-quarter acre plot to five men:

"all colored people and descendants of Africa...who are nominated trust-ees...of the B.E.M. Religious Society for their use to make a burying ground for the interment of their dead and for them to erect a meeting house for the purpose of meeting there as often as they may think proper to worship Almighty God in spirit and truth."

Besides Rev. Aquilla Scott, the trustees included Benjamin Johnson, Thomas and Joshua Harvey and Wesley Hayes. A new log church was built on the Ruxton site. The original place of worship is depicted in a primitive watercolor painting by Eliza Hawkins. She marked the drawing with the inscription: "BUILD [sic] 1835." Both slaves and free blacks attended services in the log church, later named St. John's African Union Methodist Protestant Church (AUMP).

At the time the log church was erected, an early map shows it facing north, and Bellona Avenue doglegged west and crossed the Baltimore & Susquehanna Railroad just north, then crossed the railroad just north and west of St. John's cemetery. After travelling a few hundred yards south, Bellona crossed back over the tracks and headed east up the hill toward Charles Street. Lake Roland reservoir was planned for Baltimore City's water supply and in 1853 a large portion of the Bellona Gunpowder Mills was sold to the new water works for $17,500. Still more acreage was needed for the impoundment to the east, so Bellona Avenue was straightened and moved entirely to the east side of the railroad tracks and the little log church property. Based on the early drawing of the log church, it was no larger than 12 by 18 feet seating about fifteen or twenty persons. The stone tenant farmer's house that later became the church parsonage was probably built from stone gathered from the local pastures in the late 1700s.

According to Marie Scott Brown, the earliest burials in the cemetery are those nearest the railroad tracks. Most slaves were interred without headstones, but perhaps were marked with simple wooden crosses that have rotted away. By the year 2002, many sandstone and limestone monuments had deteriorated due to weather and vandalism. In addition to the sixty names recorded by family geneal-ogist Delores B. Scott in 1983, there are probably twenty more persons interred without markers or where the stones have no inscription, been broken, buried or stolen. One stone begs for more research. It reads: In Memory of Harriett Tate/ Beloved Mother of St. John's.

William Walter Scott, III, recalls the funeral service in 1960 of his paternal grandmother, Henrietta Scott (mother of Marie Scott Brown), who was almost ninety at the time. "The church was packed, and emotions were high, since she had long been the matriarch of our clan," he said. All nine grandchildren saw her laid to rest in the cemetery between the church and parsonage next to her husband, the first William Walter Scott.

ST JOHN A U M.P CHURCH

The log church in Ruxton was depicted in this watercolor by Eliza Hawkins shortly after it was built in 1835 and later burned, replaced by the 1886 chapel.——Marie Scott Brown

Founded by Bishop Richard Allen, The African Methodist Episcopal Church (AME) was established in Maryland in 1798 after Daniel Coker, an escaped slave born on the Eastern Shore, went to New York to receive Methodist training. Then without freedom papers, he courageously came to Baltimore to preach. (In 1853, Maryland enacted a law making free blacks entering the state from the north liable to sale as slaves.) Considering several conference affiliations, St. John's board decided to join the African Union Methodist Protestant Church. Then it turned to the AME denomination and was governed out of Wilmington, Delaware, according to Marie Scott Brown, but three generations of Scotts had held the title of trustees and refused to give up its property and savings.

There were schismatic squabbles among the small African Methodist bodies in those days revealed religious scholar Lewis V. Baldwin of Vanderbilt University. St. John's Church in Ruxton changed its name, if not its affiliation, several times during its early years of existence. "Itinerancy, episcopacy and structure caused many riffs between the similar ideologies," said Professor Baldwin. "In 1865 the African Union Methodist Protestant Church (AUMP) emerged replacing their elders with presidents, but continuing to stress their roots to the African Union Church organized in 1816 by Peter Spencer of Wilmington, Delaware." In addition to St. John's, St. Andrews of Mt. Washington, St. James of East Towson, and Tyson in Cross Keys were initially AUMP denominations.

As the Industrial Revolution arrived in Maryland, copper ore was discovered at Bare Hills in 1839. In that year Aquilla Scott bought for $90 a two-acre parcel on which he built a home and his first log church. It bordered Falls Road. At the time Scott negotiated his Bare Hills land purchase, it was owned by Johnza Hook, but years before it had been part of the Thomas Hooker warrant of 1694 for 2,000 acres within the Back River-Upper Hundred and Middlesex Hundred Districts. "Hooker assigned half of this warrant to James Murray who in turn passed the acreage to Hector McClane..." and the parcel became known as *Hector's Hopyard*. According to some accounts, McClane tried tobacco as a cash crop, but hops and grains were less labor intensive and more profitable. "I remember the stuff [hops] growing wild up on a fence between our yard and the one next door," said Marie Scott Brown. "They called it hops." Colonists were using the grain for making beer, ale and malt liquor. In 1702, two hundred acres of the *Hopyard* north of Jones Falls were sold to James Carroll, grandnephew of Carroll of Carrollton. Then over the years various parcels were transferred and sold, finally according to the Assessment of 1783, a 116-acre farm in the northern section of the original *Hopyard* belonged to John Fishpaw. At his death in 1825...the land was passed to Fishpaw's son, Elijah. It was the tiny northeast corner of this parcel that was to later become the location of the original St. John's log church in Ruxton.

After twenty-five years of service, Rev. Aquilla Scott, the first pastor of St. John's, died of a heart attack at age seventy-four while preaching in the old log church. It was Sunday morning, February 28, 1858. The senior Aquilla never lived in the stone parsonage and wasn't interred at St. John's apparently choosing to be buried in the family cemetery next to his home in Bare Hills. Recognizing the need to replace the original trustees who were dying out, on May 2, 1860, St. John's was incorporated as St. John's Colored Methodist Church with nine new trustees: Thomas H. Robinson, Edward Diggs, Andrew J. Barney, William Anderson, Abraham Foote, James Bordley, Nathaniel Scott, William Moore and John Henry Garriott.

After his father's death, James Aquilla Scott, Junior, (Quill as he was known) took over as blacksmith and minister at St. John's. Marie Scott Brown says her grandfather, Aquilla, Jr., had added a little store to his Falls Road blacksmith shop. "With wagons loaded with produce and fruits from up the country," she said, "farmers might stop for repairs and buy something to drink—I think he sold beer—and something to eat. His trade benefited the traffic on the old road," said Marie.

While smithing on a farm in the Shawan and Cuba Road (Oregon Ridge) area of Baltimore County, Quill met a slave girl, Anar Gough. Descendants pronounced her name OHN-na Goff. Later he bought her from the abusive landowner. It is written in different accounts that she could speak little or no English, could neither read nor write. At the time of their marriage, about 1850, she is said to have been three years his senior and had "long blond braids." Some say she was the daughter of the white master and a slave girl on the plantation. As a miscegenation of black and white, she could have had blond hair. But not being able to speak English, it also is possible that she was a white indentured slave (servant) from Europe and Quill bought out her work contract. Further, the name *Anar* could indicate she was of Swedish descent. Quill affectionately called her Honora. They had six children and, as they grew up, Quill continued to build more homes for them in the enclave. One time in 1867, he used lumber salvaged from an old Methodist Church that had stood at Smith and Greely Avenues in Mt. Washington.

The log chapel in Ruxton burned to the ground in the 1860s, possibly from the sparks of a passing train that ignited the tinder-dry brush surrounding the church. The railroad tracks are within 120 feet of the present St. John's and the old log structure may have been closer. It was on these tracks that Abraham Lincoln passed on his way to give his famous address at Gettysburg on November 19, 1863. Less than two years later the assassinated President's body was carried over the same route to Illinois for burial. Under the direction of Aquilla Scott, Jr., a new larger St. John's chapel was built in 1886 by George Horn[e], a Towson carpenter.

The 1886 St. John's Church is a beautifully scaled, one-room American Gothic-revival building little altered from when it was built and still in good condition. It is said to have been erected on the same foundation as the old log house of worship. However, a report by architect Jim Wollon said the present foundation was built to accommodate this specific church that is "much larger than would be expected for a black congregation of the 1830s." He added that there is no indication that the earlier foundation was enlarged. Moreover, he said, "according to tradition, log structures often did not have substantial, solid stone foundations."

St. John's Chapel measures 35 feet 7 inches by 20 feet 7 inches and has board and batten siding, a steep roof originally covered in cedar shakes, fish scale shakes on both gable ends, lancet windows and louvered shutters with star dogs, "egg and dart" gingerbread trim, stained glass ornamental windows in either end and double entrance doors. There is a crawlspace under most of the foundation with support piers for the floor joists. Recently a pit, possibly used for anthracite coal storage, was discovered under the west end. Inside the church there are random width pine floors throughout the nave, hand-made pews for about seventy persons, and a raised altar with lectern and communion rail. An inscription above the altar reads: WELCOME TO ALL and was hand-lettered over an illustration of an open Bible. The church was once heated by two potbelly stoves, one in the south center of the nave, its chimney opening still visible in the ceiling. The second was on the opposite wall somewhat forward of the other stove. Electric heat has now been installed. The ceiling is raked at a lower pitch then the roof indicating a scissor-truss system. Illumination for the 1886 church was from three overhead kerosene chandeliers lowered and raised by ropes through eyebolts (still visible). There were kerosene lamps on the two posts on either side of the altar, now converted to electric. The surviving reed organ, with side trays for kerosene lamps, is an Estey "chapel" model. It cost $240 in the 1890s and originally had been located in the right front side of the altar. It is now in the back of the church waiting for a $1,500 reconditioning.

At the cornerstone laying ceremony of the 1886 church, the hollow marble box was filled with a Bible, Methodist hymnal, a copy of the Discipline of the Church, the Saturday Baltimore Sun and a list of prominent national and local personages. At three o'clock on Sunday, August 29, the stone was laid in place at the southeast corner of the foundation by Rev. Edward W. Scott, son of James Aquilla Scott, Sr. The stone reads: ST. JOHN'S A.U.M.P./CHURCH./A.D. 1886.

> The next day, the Baltimore *Sun* reported "Rev. Scott preached an excellent sermon outside in the shade of a number of large trees." It went on to say, "The church will be a pretty little frame building...situated on a hill overlooking Lake Roland, about a quarter mile above Lake Station.... A number of members of the colored lodge of the Order of the Seven Wise Men of Melvale, were in attendance."

The newspaper also noted that "Rev. E. W. Scott, a member of the founding family, preached the same evening at a camp meeting held at Paradise Grove on Merryman's Lane, somewhere near present University Parkway."

The son of James Aquilla Scott, Sr., Rev. Edward W. Scott (1841–1919) and his wife, Henrietta (1835–1880) are buried at St. John's cemetery.—Tony and Holly Parker

Anar Scott died in 1892 and Quill, Jr., in 1906. Both are buried at St. John's cemetery.

After ninety-six years, the last twenty of which St. John's Chapel had been closed to regular worship, few people took an interest in the church or, in fact, realized there were even buildings back in the tangle of weeds off Bellona Avenue. It wasn't until 1979 when Gail O'Donovan who was doing some pro bono zoning research for the local improvement association that the fortune of the neglected church began a remarkable change. An adjacent homeowner had wanted to rezone land during the 1980 Comprehensive Zoning Maps process in order to build business offices between the chapel property and Bellona Avenue.

In preparing to fight the rezoning attempt, O'Donovan was enchanted by St. John's, at the time, a deteriorating property. She researched deeds and visited the remaining church trustees, the "Scott sisters," living beyond Lake Roland in Bare Hills. "I had prayed to God to tell me what to do," said Marie Scott Brown. "And Gail O'Donovan appeared." O'Donovan also discovered that the county tax department had been over-charging the elderly sisters for two acres on Falls Road instead of three-quarters of an acre on Bellona Avenue. Eventually they were refunded three years of the decades they had already paid taxes on the church property.

Joseph M. Coale notes in his book, *Middling Planters of Ruxton,* that the entrance road to St. John's Chapel had been the old unnamed road that still runs down the gully between the present Shell station on Bellona Avenue and St. John's Chapel. In the late 1700s, the road led west to the Bellona Gunpowder Mills (now covered by Lake Roland) and later was used by the Fishpaw farm.

The "little white angel," as Gail O'Donovan was called by the Scotts, asked the sisters if they'd like her help in establishing St. John's as an historic site, preserved for all time. Both the late Esther Scott and Marie Scott Brown were delighted with her proposed ideas. The project took on the unwieldy name of "The Restoration and Preservation of Historic St. John's Church, Ruxton."

Gail O'Donovan organized a volunteer board and a committee of fundraisers. To kick off the campaign, Baltimore architect W. Boulton "Bo" and Ellen Kelly held a reception on Sunday, October 25, 1981, at their home on Bellona Avenue. It took eighteen months before the team raised $108,000 from the Merrick-France Foundation, Federal, State and County historical organizations and private citizens. O'Donovan used the organization Kelly and preservationist Bill Trimble founded, Baltimore County Historical Trust (associated with the Maryland Historical Trust), as a repository for the collected funds and pay out expenses for renovation. Most of the work force to clean up and restore the property was some fifty volunteers including Boy Scout Troops #35 and #921. "We tried to get as much work done free of charge," said Gail. "Charlie Tipper was one of the few we paid. And I think he did a wonderful job."

Tipper had just graduated from Middlebury College in Vermont and was excited to return to his hometown to work on a true historic preservation project. He was paid "a not-to-exceed figure" of $5,000 and told, by contract, to finish the restoration of St. John's Chapel in a year. "I have a special fondness for small buildings that show such an obvious connection to people and the community," said Tipper recently. He began his work in the fall of 1982, at about the time the land was surveyed. "I just started picking away at it," he said. "It hadn't been painted in many years. The outside paint was thick, alligatored and peeling. I had to scrape paint for weeks on end. We identified fourteen coats and many colors. After consulting with Tom Spies A.I.A., [volunteer architect for the job], we decided to go with the same colors that were among the first used in 1886: light gray for the main body of the chapel, ivory trim and dark green shutters.

Charlie Tipper said one of the most enjoyable challenges was repairing the two round stain glass windows in both gables, especially the one on the west end. Leaking water had damaged the outside shingles that had to be replaced along with most of the structural framing and the plaster inside. "Much of the interior back wall was dilapidated, plaster falling off," he said. "It was a mess." One day when Tom Spies came in to inspect the work he was surprised to see the west end of the church nearly open to the outside. "I just began taking out bad wood and it kept going and going," said Tipper. "Everything was rotted or eaten by the powder post beetles. "In the process, I had to remove the round frames of the stain glass windows, reconstitute them with new wood and epoxy and repair the glass off-site. Re-plastering over wooden lathes took weeks. The interior hadn't been painted much, but I put up scaffolding and went to work. In the sanctuary, artist Emily Taliaferro copied, then repainted, the lettering, WELCOME TO ALL, and the illustration of the Bible.

In 1983, a special tent was used to cover St. John's Chapel in order to fumigate destructive powder post beetles.—Charlie Tipper.

About three-quarters of the way through his work contract, the restoration fund ran out of money, so Charlie Tipper took off four months and traveled around the world. Returning to the project in April of the next year, he worked until the following September. He replaced window sash cords and stabilized the crumbling stone foundation with "a traditional mixture of sand, lime and a low concentration of Portland cement." The most worrisome part of the project, said Tipper, was the powder post beetles, *Lyctus brunneus*. "They were eating the beams and flooring," he said "and we knew the only way they could be killed was to erect a giant tent over the building and fumigate the entire structure. A posted sign read: DANGER/Fumigating with/METHYL BROMIDE/DEADLY POISON/ALL PERSONS WARNED TO KEEP AWAY. To inspect its effectiveness after the first application, Charlie spread white drop cloths in the crawlspace under the church. To his chagrin there were still piles of wood dust coming from the beams. Beetles were still alive, and he surmised it was because the first fumigation was done in cold weather. Later another fumigation did kill the beetles. After Tipper's more finish-related work was completed, other contractors installed nine additional floor joists "sistered" against damaged ones, a new electrical heating system, and lighting and outlets to meet the building codes of the day. His restoration work completed, Charlie relocated to an island in Lake Champlain, Vermont, where today he is president of the South Hero Land Trust and operates a successful building business.

On Thursday, April 29, 1982, while at the height of renovation, Governor Harry Hughes and a host of government and preservation officials visited St. John's. The governor presented a document, dated March 15, 1982, that placed St. John's on the National Register of Historic Places. He also presented a check for $8,000 from the Department of Interior and thanked the volunteers working on the project. Gail O'Donovan was recognized for her leadership. "Anyone who thinks one voice can't make a difference is proved wrong. She's made an incredible difference to the future of St. John's Church," noted one account of the event.

Ann and Lola Brown, residents of 6244 Falls Road in Bare Hills, wrote a letter to church officials on October 9, 1985, adding to the history of St. John's. Their parents, Robert "Buck" and Carrie Brown "helped build and maintain the church and were the first to be married in it. Buck promoted…dances, box parties, concerts or any form of fundraisings suitable for church affairs. These endeavors were to help defray building costs of the social hall…later converted to living quarters." The elderly sisters also mentioned "The electric lighting in the church pulpit and [at] each end of the altar, was installed and donated by a relative, Mr. Alonzo Yates. For many years he served as choir director and organist for the church." Miss Sophia Yates, an aunt of Alonzo's, and Mr. John Gardman, his wife, Minnie [Scott], and their families were among those who supported the historic church.

In addition to the church and parsonage, the social hall "bungalow," as it was called, was located at the southeast extremity of the lot, "down in the bottom," and used for socials and dances. With its dirt basement floor, it is estimated that it was probably built as a hall about the turn of the century, but later turned into a residence. Having been badly vandalized in the 1970s, preservationists determined that it was of no importance historically or architecturally and the hall was torn down in 1982.

The parsonage building was another story. It was a bigger project because vandals had torched it on the afternoon of March 23, 1981, then again two days later. Some say the publicity surrounding the restoration drew attention to the old building and its planned future. The fire gutted the inside and burned away the shed addition on the rear. Except for the four stone exterior walls, the three-room interior had to be totally rebuilt. A lot more money would be needed.

Tom Spies took charge of getting the paper work through the state in order to secure a grant. Using forensic techniques, a comprehensive Historic Structure Report was prepared by Jim Wollon, A.I.A. According to the Havre de Grace architect, details within the charred parsonage debris indicated that the structure was probably standing on the parcel when it was deeded in 1833, having been built much earlier as a tenant farmhouse. This was contrary to popular belief. Once used as the minister's residence, the parsonage measures 20 feet 7 inches across the front and 18 feet 3 inches deep. Wollom discovered scarifications of a large fireplace in the middle of the south wall, the 7 feet 3 inch chimneybreast being built entirely inside the wall. An enclosed spiral staircase leading to the second floor was squeezed into the southwest corner. There had been another smaller fireplace on the second level. A very large out-of-scale dormer had been located on the front slope of the roof, but cost and taste prevented it from being rebuilt. Anyway, it was determined the scorched roof had been replaced with machine cut wood and wire nails as late as the twentieth century.

"Renovating the parsonage was an arduous task, but we were energized," said Spies. "Finally with state approval and money in hand, we put the project out for bid. Hugh Andrews, a very good local homebuilder, got the job to do the cedar shake roofing and framing for $50,000. First tenant in the parsonage was the new director of Chesapeake Habitat for Humanity who had just arrived in town and had his organization help with much of the interior partitions, drywall, painting and finish work in exchange for free rent. The parsonage was completed and occupied within three months.

Several years later in March 1998, a young Janet and Paul Reynolds moved into the house as caretakers in exchange for a reduction in rent. "It was a wonderful place to live," Janet exclaimed. "We loved it and so did our Golden Retriever. We stayed there for nearly three years." As an architect, she described the interior. "The front door enters into a central living room with deep-set windows. Stair steps on the right went to the second floor bedroom. There was one small window on the south side, but a three by four foot skylight filtered in additional light. You had to be careful if it rained. And if you had the skylight opened while you were sleeping, whenever the light rail train passed by, it sounded like it was coming right through the room." Once when a mini-tornado went through, one of those big walnut trees came down striking the bedroom roof. Fortunately only the highest branches of the two-foot thick tree hit, so there was hardly any damage. Just a lot of noise. Janet continued her depiction of the inside of the downstairs. "In the rear, there is a galley kitchen and a full bath. It really was an enjoyable place to live," she concluded.

*Detail of an early aerial photograph of Ruxton shows St. John's Chapel **1**, parsonage **2**, social hall **3**, Northern Central Railway **4**, Bellona Avenue **5**, road to Fishpaw Farm, **6**, cemetery **7**.—Sally Willse*

Toward the end of 2002, an old aerial photograph of Ruxton turned up showing St. John's Chapel, the parsonage and social hall. Sally G. Willse found the torn and soiled photograph in the second floor den of her home in Ruxton. She explained: "This is the house my late father built and as I was organizing some of the items Dad had left, I discovered the aerial view in a drawer of pictures and realized it was of Ruxton. It had to have been taken about 1922 or 1923 because it shows my grandfather David Barton, Sr.'s house under construction across Ruxton Road. I guess the picture came over here when my grandmother, Sally, switched houses with my parents."

A benchmark stone, with its "X" clearly visible, indicates the northeast corner of the *Hector's Hopyard* tract. It still rests a hundred feet north of the present St. John's Church on the entrance road off Bellona Avenue. It should be mentioned that the present entrance road and parking area cover a number of early graves. Today St. John's Chapel is listed as a Baltimore County Landmark. A roadside marker on Bellona Avenue tells the story and uses its official name from the 1860 deed: "The Colored Methodist Protestant St. John's Chapel of Baltimore County."

Carolyn Scott LeVere places flowers at the grave of Aquilla Scott, Sr., her great grandfather, in the family cemetery in Bare Hills.

Carolyn Scott LeVere periodically visits her great grandfather Aquilla Sr.'s grave in the Scott family cemetery in Bare Hills. Its marker is a slab of limestone laying flat among the grasses. Unfortunately its carved inscriptions are deteriorating and becoming difficult to read: "In memory of/REVD AQUILLA SCOTT/ the minister who passed away/while in prayer/in the church below/now joins/the church above/February 28th/1858." Aquilla's grave, and those of twin sons who died at birth, are located in the quiet glade among fruit trees close to the dilapidated remains of his former residence. William Walter Scott, Jr., a current Bare Hills resident, believes there are at least six or eight unmarked graves in this cemetery.

The home of Aquilla Scott, Sr., was the first built in the Bare Hills enclave, c. 1840. It burned in the mid-1950s and, while still standing, is in need of immediate renovation.

Historically, the most important dwelling in the Scott settlement in Bare Hills is that of Aquilla, Sr. It's a shake-sided frame home with two dormers and a standing metal-over-shake roof and brick chimney. Carolyn Scott LeVere used to live there. She remembers as a twelve-year-old coming home from a social function one night in January 1956. The car in which she rode was heading south on Falls Road. Rounding a curve she saw ahead the red sky and flashing lights from the fire engines. Once parked, young Carolyn ran among the snaking hoses trying to get closer, but the fire already had burned the southwest corner of the home. Although the remains were still sizzling, she convinced a fireman to go inside and retrieve her purse from under the bed. Carolyn said she thought the fire was arson, retribution for an adulterous family relationship. The historic house still stands, but is vine covered, tottering and will soon crumble to the ground, if not saved.

Over the years, the St. John's Church property was bought and sold to various individuals and corporations. Squabbles and other problems beset the congregation, and one deed says Aquilla Phillips and his wife, Priscilla Scott Phillips, a daughter of William Scott, purchased the land November 30, 1865 for $600 from Lewis J. Roberts and Amia E. Roberts, his wife, white landowners of the Ruxton area. At the time, remains of the log church were just a pile of charred wood within a depression of the flooring. Ultimately in 1866 ownership of the property went to Aquilla Scott, Jr., and his heirs. Twenty years later, Scott supervised the building of the new St. John's. Although the present Scott family will remain the owners of the church "forever," the nine trustees gave a "Deed of Easement" to the Baltimore County Historical Trust on October 26, 1992 to ensure perpetual protection of the property. The grantors were Anna Marie Scott Brown, Beulah Scott, Delores Scott, Asbury Rideout, Lucy Bond, Carolyn Scott LeVere, Viola Rideout, Doretha Davis Carr and Thomas W. Davis.

The junior Aquilla Scott was the older brother of Rev. Edward W. Scott, who laid the cornerstone at St. John's. In 1885 Edward also was active in building St. Andrew's AUMP Church on Western Run in Mt. Washington. When fire destroyed the original St. Andrew's Church in 1918, the congregation was forced to use a nearby abandoned Baptist Church. Landowner Martha Townsend deeded a parcel for the second St. Andrew's that was constructed in 1926 and still stands. After cessation of services in the late 1960s, it was first used as a recreation center, and now has been converted into a private residence on the south side of Kelly Avenue. Rev. Edward Scott also was pastor of St. James Church in East Towson, and founder and pastor of the Tyson AUMP Church in Cross Keys Village, and it is said later became a bishop.

5

The Island Village

Cross Keys Village was an island of African American families surrounded by a vast ocean of whites. There continued to be inequality between the races except when white men were attracted to black girls and women. It was well known that white politicians often visited the Cross Keys Inn and Arthur and Bettie Scott's beer garden cafe, opposite one another on Falls Road. "Scotty's," or "Miss Bettie's, as it was better known, was run by Bettie Scott. It had a beer garden on the ground floor with entertainment for the politicians including gambling. On the second floor was a rooming house and more entertainment. Arthur was a son of Rev. Edward W. Scott.

During prohibition, Douglas Grant Scott, M.D., another son of Rev. Scott, would leave his home at 4711 Falls Road in Cross Keys and visit his brother's nearby cafe to give "medication" to any needy pols. "And if they were in such a state," said descendant Tony Parker, "they may have a lady look after them on the second floor." In his practice, Dr. Scott had to perform abortions in the village and it is said he buried fetuses in back of his house. Later, Dr. Scott moved his offices and residence to 354 West Biddle Street. "After he moved downtown, he still returned to treat residents several times a week," said Jerry Hynson. "For emergencies, we'd have to take the patient to the back door of Dr. Henry F. Cassidy, a white physician, who lived at 1 Upland Road in Roland Park. It was free for African Americans and we didn't mind that we only got a few minutes because he always had a roomful of paying white patients waiting." Dr. Scott became the first "Negro physician to receive privileges at Johns Hopkins Hospital." He died June 13, 1952 at age 84.

Marie Scott Brown tells the story of one married, well-to-do white man who impregnated a black woman. At birth, he and his wife took the newborn and raised her. "As a baby they treated Miss Carrie like their own," said Marie, "but as she got older, and darker, they couldn't take her to certain places unless they passed her off as their servant girl, which they did. When all members of the prominent family had died and the houses were sold, Miss Carrie was said to have inherited a substantial sum, but sadly was sent south, I believe to Virginia or North Carolina, to live with some cousins," she said. "I took her to the train station. Later I heard they mistreated her, and she died of a broken heart"

Parker Douglass, son of slaves, operated a popular grocery store in Cross Keys Village and lived above it with his wife. He died at the age of 104. The brick structure still stands next to the south end of ManorCare at 4639 Falls Road.—Vertelle Hall.

Twenty years ago at age 104, Parker Berkley Douglass, Jr., was the oldest person living in Cross Keys Village and was, according to Jerry Hynson, a descendant of Frederick Douglass. Margaret Doyle said recently that while she was head of the English department at Robert Poole Middle School in the late 1970s she had specifically asked that question of Mr. Douglass and he said he was not related. It is possible that Douglass didn't know of his relationship with his distinguished black kin. Doyle's two-year project captured the Cross Keys history on an illustrated filmstrip and was to be used throughout the city school system. Unfortunately the work has been lost.

Douglass was the son of slaves. "My father was separated from his parents," he said in an early interview. "As a slave, he had no education. Slept on the ground. So many people were bought and sold, just like animals," said Douglass. "He didn't know much about his mother, but said his father once walked fifty miles to see him when he was twelve. "He told me about seeing Confederate soldiers during the Civil War in Richmond eating bread out of the gutter. I'll never forget that. Then I never saw him again."

Douglass was born in 1879 at Powhattan (Woodlawn), Maryland. Rutherford B. Hayes was president and pulling out Federal troops from the occupied South at the end of the Reconstruction Era. Douglass was the youngest of seven children. His mother died when he was two. "I went to a one-room school house and I guess I was about 10 when I finished the second grade and quit. In those days, children were older in the grades. I did learn to read, write and do some arithmetic.

"People weren't so much interested in education when I was a boy. When I was fifteen, I went to work for my stepfather driving horses. We hauled bricks, sand and clay for ten cents a load." At the time he was living in South Baltimore. Around the age of 20, Parker worked at the Charles Street sanitarium in the 2700 block Charles Street. While there he was offered a job to work at *Maple Hill*, a mansion then owned by Robert Poole, the son of a wealthy Woodberry manufacturer on whose property the mansion and later, the Robert Poole Middle School were built. In later life, Parker Douglass became a volunteer at the school.

When he was twenty-five, the Great Baltimore Fire broke out in 1904 and he personally viewed the devastation. "I lived at the top of the hill in the Gwynns Falls-Wetheredsville (now Dickeyville) area." A few years later he moved near Falls Road when it was little more than a dirt path through farmland and the only means of transportation was by foot, horse or carriage. A telephone company two-horse team got stuck in the mud for two days, he recalled. "Everybody 'round here had chickens and hogs," he said. "Just down the road was a tollgate and the only thing that passed up and down was a four-mule team from Rockland Mill."

Douglass and third wife, Mary May Street, moved to Cross Keys Village. In 1905 the Douglasses had their first child, Carl, and some years later had another son who died at age 28. During World War I, Douglass, 37, worked in a munitions factory. Through the efforts of Mrs. Douglass, who bargained for the land, a two-story brick house was built at 4639 Falls Road next to the Falls Road AME

Church. They opened the basement as a grocery store in 1930 and operated it seven days a week until 1968. "He was a lovely man," said Marie Brown. "I was a shy young woman and felt more comfortable buying my things from his wife, Miss Douglass. She was nice, too."

"Pork chops were ten cents a pound and we didn't have ten cents," Douglass recounted in a Michael Olesker column in the *Sun*. He retired from the store when he was eighty-nine, but continued to drive his car until his late nineties. Married for forty years, Parker's wife, Mary May, died in 1952.

At his centennial celebration, Douglass was said to look forty years younger, not a wrinkle in his face. He was a diminutive, dapper man with white hair who wore gold wire-rimmed glasses and a hearing aid. When he walked, he used a cane. After his wife passed, he lived alone and independent in his home on Falls Road where he died in 1983.

Douglass undoubtedly knew Caroline Hammond, born in 1844, the young daughter of a slave woman. The two women were both owned by Thomas Davidson, a farmer in Anne Arundel County. In 1938, Mrs. Hammond lived in Cross Keys Village at 4710 Falls Road where she was interviewed by Page Harris, a government sponsored writer. It was the same dwelling that was later occupied by Jerry Hynson's family. Mrs. Hammond's mother was a house slave that gave her privileges. She supervised all the cooking and her brother Billie was [a butler] "dressed in a uniform decorated with brass buttons, braid and a fancy vest, his hands encased in white gloves" as he shook the tiny dinner bell to announce dinner.

"Mother," she said, "with the consent of Mr. Davidson, married George Berry, a free colored man of Annapolis. He was a carpenter and was to buy mother within three years of marriage for $750. Payment could be made periodically. Unfortunately Mr. Davidson was accidentally killed while duck hunting on South River. While father had only $40 more to pay on mother's account, Mrs. Davidson refused to honor the agreement and mother and I had to remain slaves.

"Father, being well-known and free, was able to arrange for mother and me to escape to Baltimore. The three of us sheltered with a white family on Ross Street on our long trip on the underground railroad. One day we were placed in a covered wagon driven by Mr. Coleman's six horses through different villages along the turnpike to Hanover, Pennsylvania. We never stopped close to any settlement because, by then, a $100 reward had been placed on us by Mrs. Davidson and the Anne Arundel sheriff. We continued our trip north finally arriving at Scranton, Pennsylvania, where my parents were both employed by the same family for a total of $27.50 per month."

Caroline Hammond and her family returned to Baltimore in 1869 and she entered the seventh grade in south Baltimore. She and her husband, George, moved to Cross Keys Village. He died in 1927 at age 84. Although she was interviewed when she was 94, there is no later reference to Caroline's death.

When it was built, a half-century before Caroline Hammond was born, Cross Keys Inn was out in the county hinterlands, far from the Baltimore City limits that ended at a North Avenue barbed wire fence. Sometime before 1850, the inn was owned by two brothers—John and William Mather and John's wife. An 1852 map by Thomas P. Chiffelle shows "Tavern" and "M. Mather" on the west side of Falls Road near the tollgate at Coldspring Lane.

The proprietors of the place have been many. One of the Mather brothers, the one who was married, died. The surviving brother married the widow and then he too died. Then the widow ran the place for herself a while. Later she married George Washington.

Washington was a white Englishman who was brought to this country as an indentured coachman by William "Billy" McDonald, a wealthy bon vivant who lived in "Guilford," a fifty-room Italianate mansion built on 296-acres by his father on the York Road (now Guilford). Junior was owner of the famous trotting mare, "Flora Temple" (c.1859) which was so admired that he often showed her off to guests in his palatial marbled parlor. Before he married, Washington is said to have had a relationship with a black Scott woman and bore him several children.

One of Tony Parker's cousins, who lives near Greenmount Cemetery, told him that her great grandfather was a white British coachman named Washington and "I am the great granddaughter of that British coachman," she said emphatically. "She was very light skinned," recalled Parker. Oral history says that when Washington died, Cross Keys Inn was bought by Perry Knight, a member of a large family in Heathbrook and Woodberry. His brother was a policeman in Roland Park.

In 1884 prominent citizens had the state legislature pass a local-option bill that allowed the take-over of the land on which the tavern rested and it was turned into a roadhouse. Situated in the heart of the Ninth District, it became a popular gathering place for Baltimore County politicians. Congressman J. Fred C. Talbott, Dr. James Maddox, James F. Busey, Charles Goodman were among many others who would convene to watch cock fights among feathery contestants from many states. The Cross Keys Inn, then a tavern and rooming house, was sold at a sheriff's sale in September 1895 for $800 to William Tunney. "It was a rather disreputable Irish place," said William Hollifield, author of a history of turnpikes in Baltimore City and County. "Respectable people would tend to stay away from a place like that."

When Perry Knight died in 1887, his obituary stated, "He was particularly fond of fast horses and game chickens" and "one of the best wing shots in the country." Incidentally, it may be remembered "Perry's Ordinary" became the name of the lounge in James Rouse's Cross Keys Inn, a hundred years later.

Much of Cross Keys Village at the turn of the nineteenth century was owned by the Charles Bakers, Gillet Gills and Anton Spaths. The Bakers owned property from Coldspring Lane, the commencement of the village, up to Ridgewood Road and back to the Gill holdings, which were in the middle of the village. The Gills owned a strip right back of their home on Ridgewood Road. Spath...who lived further up on Falls Road, owned all the rest, and was the principal landholder. (Later, Simon Scott, Jr., was a large speculator in Cross Keys land and houses.)

The oldest family in Cross Keys Village was the Baker family. It included the widow of Charles H. Baker, founder of the dairy, a son Davis Baker, later proprietor of the dairy, a Miss Baker, who lived with her mother on Coldspring Lane, and O. Parker Baker, a Baltimore attorney. Mrs. Baker's father, Samuel Davis, was an associate of Jesse Tyson, who began to mine the copper deposits at Bare Hills on a large scale in 1864.

On the other side of the Falls Turnpike from the inn was White Oak Grove, with its name emblazoned on its entrance gate. It had a dance pavilion with polished floor tucked among huge oak trees and had brass bands and fiddlers playing on special occasions and Saturday nights during the warmer months. A spacious green lawn led south to the home of O. Parker Baker who died in the early 1920s. Between his home (which was later torn down and replaced by Elburn's filling station) and the Grove lay a "landmark and phenomenon, a gnarled and misshapen oak tree, prone to the ground, its trunk and branches stretching fifty feet horizontally." When reported in *The Evening Sun* in 1934, "the tree had already borne blossoms and leaves for forty years," but probably was an early victim of the paving of a service station parking lot.

Left, *June Hawkins in front of Elburn's gas station once located on the east side of Falls Road, just south of White Oak Grove (now CVS Pharmacy). George N. Brown, sometimes called the "Mayor" of Cross Keys Village, was custodian of School 158.*——Paul Johnson

For special parties at White Oak Grove, a small booth supplied liquid refreshment from the inn. In some of the earliest newspaper accounts, there was another cockfighting ring in the corner of the Grove. The tavern and Grove were said to be the most notable entertainment features of the village.

Vertelle Hawkins Hall, 73, who was raised at 4656 Falls Road, remembers the Grove's spring-fed pond. When it froze over in winter her brother, family and friends would take to ice skates. "In the summer time there were gold fish swimming in the pond," she said. She also learned to play softball with her sisters and cousins using the trees as bases. Entertainment took many forms in Cross Keys, yet there were no movie theaters. Occasionally the Recreation Department would bring some boxing matches for us to watch at the school," said John McBride. "I can still see Joe Lewis and Billy Conn going at it."

But who could forget Paul Johnson giving one of his "plays" for the local children? As a youth, Paul would get his material by hiking to the Harlem Movie Theater on Gilmor Street. He'd practically memorize the film's dialog and when he got home he'd rehearse while creating sets, sound effects and costumes. A little child might come to the door and say, "Miss Ann, can Paul come out now and give us a play? *Ta-Da!* Out would come Paul to start his version of the movie. "There was a hill across Oakdale from our house and the younger children would sit there and watch," said Paul. "I had the entire front porch for my acts and an appreciative audience. I think it was the beginning of my school teaching career."

"The Browns were the first in the neighborhood to get a television," said John McBride. "Their grandson, Jesse Hawkins, bought it for them. It was a little ten-inch black and white, but it was wonderful and we were allowed to watch the Pabst Blue Ribbon fights through the porch window screen on Friday nights. Once we were so cold, the rest of the gang went home shivering, but I wanted to see the end. Mr. Brown noticed that I was the only one still outside and invited me to come in and get warm. "From then on," said McBride, "I had one of the best seats in the house."

"Cross Keys residents used two walking paths to get to work in Roland Park," said freckle-faced Vertelle Hall, once called "Reds" because of her flame-colored hair. "One path began at the east end of Spath Lane," she explained, "where it led up the steep slope to Roland Park and continued over to Roland Avenue." On Sunday outings, Ann Carter and her family would climb the path and go to Morgan & Millard pharmacy for ice cream cones. Also, Vertelle said there was a mountain of steps above the tennis courts at the curve of Hillside Road, another shortcut to Roland Avenue.

*At a Brown family dinner in Cross Keys Village, seated left to right, Garfield,
Lydia, George N., Ida; standing, Reita and Mildred Bryant, John, Suzie,
Benjamin, Samuel, Charles and Ruth—Vertelle Hall*

Before their marriage, Vertelle's grandparents, George N. and Mary Frances
were both named Brown, but not related. They owned the Falls Road home in
which Vert lived. She attended School No.158 several doors up the street, then
went on to Booker T. Washington and Douglass. Marie Scott Brown is her aunt
by marriage and Vertelle looks after her as if she were her own mother.

Another former resident of the old village is Delores Harvey Silva. Her mother
was a Lee. Over the years, the Harvey family lived at 4660, 4675, 4658 and
4630. When she was eight, Delores became a member of Falls Road AME
Church and attended grammar school at No.158. In her youth she took trips to
see relatives and acquaintances in Bare Hills and Mt. Washington and went shopping by trolley to the 36th Street stores.

When Delores married Otto Silva, they moved to Spath Lane in Cross Keys
Village. Vertelle Hall and Delores Silva have remained lifelong friends. Both are
interested in their forebears. "My grandfather, George N. Brown, used to tell me
about the buggies pulling up to the old Cross Keys Inn," said Mrs. Hall. "It
sounded very exciting."

On a blustery night January, 28, 1909, the Baltimore *Sun* reported that the old Cross Keys Tavern, by then turned into a residence, burned and "all that remains of the once-famous hostelry are the two end walls, which were of brick, all of the rest of the building being of frame. Several occupants of the house had narrow escapes from being caught in the building. Fortunately for them, Mrs. Edward Keys, who lives near the old house, saw the flames as they burst from the terra-cotta chimney, and rushing to the door aroused the residents. Mrs. Theodore Lang, who occupied a section of the house with her father-in-law, was in the kitchen at the time, but was not aware that the house was on fire until informed by Mrs. Keys. They left the house at once, and Mrs. Keys, then ran up to the next floor to notify Mrs. John Lessner and her two daughters—Mamie and Annie—who lived in that part of the house. All reached the outside of the building safely, although scantily clad."

The *Sun* continued, "While Mrs. Keys was busy arousing the occupants of the burning building, her son Lawrence, although suffering from rheumatism, ran to the nearest fire-alarm box and notified the fire department. The Roland Park, Mount Washington, Govanstown and Arlington departments responded to the call. After vainly trying to save the old building they turned their attention to the nearby property, which was in great danger of being burned. Several times the adjoining buildings caught fire from flying embers, but were put out before they had gained much headway. The building and most of its contents were consumed. The loss is estimated at $3,000. By a strange coincidence the former owner's son, Capt. Perry Knight of the Roland Park Fire Department, was at the fire yesterday. He was born in the house and lived there for a number of years." Damage was reported at $4,800.

The origin of the fire was never determined, but some thought the inn's time had come. At the blackened site, a residential dwelling was built on the same foundation. It fronted on the Falls Road over one hundred feet and was bounded by a hedge. The new house was built by a white family named Lessinger said Jesse Hawkins although the name could have been the Mrs. John Lessner mentioned above. It was a large frame two-story with a sloping roof and a comfortable veranda around its eastern and southern sides. Over its front door, a stained glass transom displayed two colorful crossed keys with a sword running up the middle, according to Jesse Hawkins who had been impressed by the sign with its reference to the inn and the past.

Some years later, brick row homes, similar to those in nearby Hampden, began to spring up in Cross Keys Village along West Coldspring Lane, but old-timers never felt they belonged to the village.

With a lack of masonry buildings, fires had always plagued the village throughout its history. Another fire was reported in the *Sun,* September 19, 1948: "Cross Keys, a small village on the Falls Rd., north of Cold spring La., was visited by fire early yesterday morning and before the flames could be subdued six 2-story frame dwellings were destroyed."

With the inclusion of a curving interchange of the Jones Falls Expressway at Coldspring Lane, plans were being drawn by the city's urban renewal agency to condemn and demolish all the homes of Cross Keys Village including the newest brick row homes and those on the west side of Falls Road from Coldspring to 4724 (Hillside Road) and 4501 through 4505 on the east side.

Looking north on Falls Road in the heart of the African American Cross Keys Village, c. 1950.—Enoch Pratt Library

In a report by Frank P. L. Somerville in *The Sunday Sun,* October 8, 1961, "The city allocated $197,370 for the purchase of 31 properties. Three of the parcels are unimproved. The disposition of the other properties await negotiations. Of 32 properties in the interchange area, a price had been agreed upon for nineteen, with the Federal Government sharing 50 percent of the cost.

"The urban renewal agency has paid $1,100 toward the moving expenses of twelve families." The *Sun* article went on: "The occupants of the predominantly Negro section of the north end of Cross Keys have for the most part moved either to the Forest Park and Ashburton areas or to the neighborhood of Morgan State College.

"The white residents of the southern end of the clearance area have concentrated in the Belair Road section of Northeast Baltimore. Three of the fam ilies moved out of the city—as far south as Cape St. Claire and as far north as Upperco, Md.

"Of the Negro families, an urban renewal spokesman noted that 'there is not a single one who is not far better off than in the old location.' Half of this group is buying new homes. Four members of the renewal staff have been working full-time on this relocation project since an initial survey last June."

Top left, clockwise: *Charles Graham, who lived in house #40, stands in Falls Road with Simon and Estelle Scott's house #20 in background. (See Cross Keys Village map in Appendix.)*—Paul Johnson
Ethel Scott Addison, wife of "Josey" standing where there had been a baseball field and an orchard in Bare Hills. Kleenize Cleaners at 6300 Falls Road now occupies the site.—Marie Scott Brown
Left to right: "Freddy," a visitor from Virginia, Mary Johnson, Paul Johnson and Margaret Hughes sit on front steps of house #6. (See Cross Keys Village map in Appendix.)—Paul Johnson

We wonder by what criteria the urban renewal spokesman made his judgment. By chance, did he ever live in Cross Keys Village? Did he know any of its people? Did he raise a family there, make lifelong friends, tell stories, celebrate births, graduations, marriages and deaths? Cross Keys Village was unique because of the character of those who made it a warm little settlement of black and white human beings. "Not the same blood, but family," added Ed Chaney. "Some residents were destined for great things, others like most of us, benefited from just living through the experience of community." The 200-year-old Cross Keys Village will never come again, but it is too valuable in human terms to merely translate into a modern collection of commercial buildings where the memories are turned off with the lights.

6

The Modern Urban Community is Born

Catherine Carroll Harper's farmland, known as Oakland, was given to her in 1804 as a belated marriage gift by her father, Charles Carroll of Carrollton. In those days the male, in this case her husband Robert Goodloe Harper, was to take the land, add parcels and build a manor house suitable for the display of family wealth. Robert and Kitty's land ran from the crest of Roland Avenue down the hillside and across the valley to the quirky Jones Falls. Part of this land became the first golf course of the Baltimore Country Club and was waiting for the hand of developer James Wilson Rouse to create The Village of Cross Keys.

After Jim Rouse's discharge from the U. S. Navy at the end of World War II, he and his wife Libby moved into a small community near Roland Park. Their first home was at 503 Wingate Road, a block south of Coldspring Lane. It was a comfortable two-story brick dwelling with a hip roof, covered entry and a fireplace. Two of his Navy friends, Churchill "Tink" Carey and Richard Thomas, became neighbors.

Jim had been anxious to get back to the mortgage banking business he and his partner, Hunter Moss, had started in 1939. More relaxed than usual, Jim occasionally enjoyed stretching his legs by walking from his Charles Street offices to Tyson Street, the colorful artist colony where owners, mostly Maryland Institute students, were restoring their homes into historic gems. There he met Betty Cooke, the jewelry designer and manufacturer. She used her first floor at 903 Tyson to sell her work, Japanese folk art and other objet d'art. After a number of visits, Jim asked Betty and her husband, Bill Steinmetz, also a designer, to establish a design-sense that became a hallmark of Rouse shopping centers. From those early ties and through most of Jim Rouse's career, Betty and Bill were his design consultants and confidants.

Returning war veterans were creating an increased housing demand and the Moss-Rouse Company was well positioned to benefit from the government-financed boom that lasted for a decade. In the next sixteen years, the company's mortgage loan portfolio would rise to $885 million for about seventy life insurance companies, bank pension funds and other lenders. For just the mortgage-servicing portion of the company, revenues were $1.4 million.

The company opened in the Morris Building on Charles Street, later moved down the street to suite 209 in the Fidelity Building. Its offices were then displaced by the new Veterans Administration and had to move to space in the Public Bank Building on Calvert Street. In 1946, with the returning members of the company requiring more space, Moss-Rouse bought a building at 345 St. Paul Street where it remained until 1954. Growing so fast, the partners decided to divide the company into six departments: Tink Carey headed residential mortgages, commercial financing by Larry Naylor, industrial financing by Albert "Bob" Keidel, appraisal and inspection by Harry Batchelor, mortgage service and accounting by George Stillson and research and development by Bill Rouse (who had just joined the company as a vice president) and Charles "Chilli" Jenkins. Then the company bought the Piper & Hill mortgage portfolio and a new headquarters building at 14 West Saratoga Street.

Top left, clockwise: *The late Ned Daniels who, in the early days, guided the style of The Village of Cross Keys. This photograph was taken at Riverwalk in New Orleans in 1986. Many Rouse company characteristics such as the use of organic colors and live trees in the courts of malls were Ned's ideas.*
W. Boulton "Bo" Kelly worked for Jim Rouse while in Harvard graduate school and later as a contract architect.
Betty Cooke, renowned jewelry designer and manufacturer and her husband, Bill Steinmetz. They own and operate The Store Ltd., one of the first shops in the Cross Keys Village Square.

As part of the Moss-Rouse mortgage banking business, the company was now arranging financing for commercial real estate projects, including apartments and various retail stores. "I was becoming frustrated with the limitations of the business," said Jim in his autobiography. "We were creating deals for developers, who would make a lot of money, and we would get paid a fee for arranging the financing. We had little influence over the purpose, the utility, the design, or the quality of the project."

At the turn of the decade, Jim was approached by Alexander Brown Griswold, III, to do a study of the "Mondawmin" family estate built in 1849. He had recently inherited it from his grandfather, financier Alexander Brown. It was in an interracial area of West Baltimore. After lengthy research it was decided to move ahead on a regional shopping center. According to Rouse, "The family [Griswold], and Baltimore builder Harry Bart would [each] own forty-five percent. Our company would own ten percent.

"It was during the Mondawmin project, in 1954, that I bought out Hunter Moss's share in the Moss-Rouse Company and it was renamed James W. Rouse & Company, Incorporated," wrote Jim in his unpublished autobiography. Hunter Moss is said to have wanted to start his own real estate appraisal firm, but in reality he said Jim, with his "inner intensity," had been setting up too many new corporations. "It was driving my accountant crazy," said Moss. "And," he added, "I'd never again have a lawyer as a partner." When Moss withdrew from the company, his fifty percent ownership was sold in five ten percent bundles at $30,000 each to Bob Keidel, Larry Naylor, Tink Carey and Bill Rouse. The remaining ten percent was divided and sold to other key executives in the new firm.

Here was Jim Rouse, age forty, about to become a developer. Mondawmin would result in the company's first entry into the development business, but only as the owner's representative, for the creation of a new concept in a regional shopping center. "I was in a real quandary as to how to proceed," Jim wrote. "Failure would sink, not only the venture, but the company as well. One day I was sitting on a platform with the president of City Investment Company in New York, Robert Dowling. As we were waiting turns to speak, I told him my problem with Mondawmin and he suggested creating a board of design. "Bring in the best people you can find, pay them by the day, and agree to nothing further. You will mine their knowledge so you will know what to do, and in the process, you will find out who is the most helpful. Then you can sign up one as an architect, another as a planner and so on."

"Dowling's advice would prove to be some of the best I ever received," said Jim. "Upon my return from New York, we set up a board of design for Mondawmin. It met every three weeks for seven months." Ultimately the shopping center was designed by Pietro Belluschi, dean of architecture at M.I.T., and Fisher, Nes and Campbell. "We thought we should have an enclosed mall," Rouse told Gurney Breckenfeld in *Columbia and the New Cities,* but we lost our nerve." The forty-six acre Mondawmin was to be built as a Roman Galleria, a very popular design in Europe. It was a four-sided structure with an open atrium or courtyard arranged with retail stores on two levels so shoppers could move to them among carefully landscaped gardens. An ornamental pool and a forty-foot sculptured tower added drama to the retail concept.

It was not fully leased when it opened in October 1956. Soon after, however, the Mondawmin concept caught on and was copied around the country. It is unfortunate the company went a million dollars over budget by building a seldom-used truck tunnel for store deliveries. Jim said: "We didn't have anywhere near a million dollars to pay those bills. And we didn't know where we could get it."

Two years later, on opening day of Charlottetown in North Carolina, "we gave Harry Bart, the builder, silver mugs and an engraved silver platter thanking him for finishing the project 'on time and within budget.' Thirty days later, when final costs of air conditioning, heating, electrical work and other utilities trickled in, we discovered that it was actually a million dollars over budget." Brother Bill flew to Charlotte to see if his unhappy contractors would give the company six more months to pay. They agreed and during that period, Rouse sold part ownership in Charlottetown to a Middle Eastern banking family that had relocated to the United States. Together with cutbacks in landscaping at Mondawmin, all bills were paid.

In restructuring the company for the future, Jim decided to form a public subsidiary, Community Research and Development, Inc. (CRD) which would shield the mortgage company from liabilities and, at the same time, raise capital for major shopping center development. CRD became a consolidation of Rouse, Harry Bart and Jack Meyerhoff shopping centers into a single corporation. With the help of Alex Brown and Dillon, Reed, CRD was listed over-the-counter and raised three million dollars in 1957 by selling six percent convertible debentures. Meyerhoff became chairman of the board of directors that, among others, included Bart and three of Jim's friends from the war: Augie Belmont, Sam Neel and Lee Loomis.

About that time, a new Rouse center was being planned for a five-acre site in Easton, Maryland, Jim's birthplace. It would be financed by CRD together with financial partner, Jack Meyerhoff. Named Talbottown, it was designed as a contemporary structure by Baltimore architect Alex Cochran, but changed when Jim's sister, Lydia "Dia" Pascault (pronounced Paca), and the entire Women's

Garden Club of Talbot County Civic Committee turned down the proposed "sheet glass and steel" structure, as it was later described by member Polly Shannahan.

After the lively public meeting broke up at the Tidewater Inn, the ladies sent the Rouse architects to St. Michaels to see "Crooked Intention," Vida Van Lennep's eighteenth century estate "to get an idea of what might fit in our town," said Mrs. Shannahan. "The pitch of the roof had to be more in harmony with the other historic structures in Easton." Rouse finally capitulated and completed the L-shaped Talbottown that opened March 14, 1957. Built as a Rouse investment development, Jim disclosed there was a "short time when bankruptcy was more of a deep personal dilemma than anyone wishes to consider."

In an equity partnership with Albert Stark, Harry Bart and Jack Meyerhoff, CRD undertook several other small strip centers. Waverly Tower in north Baltimore was called the "nation's first commercial urban renewal project." Another Rouse center was built near Johns Hopkins Hospital.

Using the same partnership arrangement, a year later came Harundale Mall in Glen Burnie, nine miles south of Baltimore. "We had hired Rogers, Taliaferro, Kostritsky and Lamb (RTKL) to design Harundale," said Ned Daniels, a former Rouse Company vice president and project manager. "Within the center, Hochschild, Kohn officials hired California architect Victor Gruen to design their department store. "It was one of those long-distance design jobs," said Daniels.

"I can remember that center vividly," he said. "Things were new and very exciting. We had this freedom to create. As an example, I needed some dramatic plantings for the interior and went to Pennock Florists in Philadelphia and bought several palm trees, quite big, fifty feet high, and we planted them in the middle of the mall and Jim Rouse said hesitatingly, 'Oh, if that's what you think this place needs.' Naturally he had an eye on the bottom line, but he never wanted to stifle peoples' ideas."

At one end of Harundale was a supermarket, at the other end was the department store. Under the tower, there still remains the dated signature block of concrete unveiled at the dedication. "Still there, but no longer surrounded by beautiful landscaping," lamented its designer Betty Cooke, forty-five years later. "It's just *there*," she said.

The affable Jim Rouse was always available to promote his malls. Here he attended the grand opening of Chequers men's store in Talbottown in the early 1980s.

"Jim was particularly thrilled about Harundale because it was CRD's first enclosed climate-controlled center," said Daniels, "and we were in competition with Southdale in Minneapolis which eventually won the title of *First*. The architect for Southdale was Victor Gruen who became known as the godfather of the enclosed shopping center. He was an arrogant Austrian, but renowned for his creations in the Midwest. Just before Harundale opened, Jim heard that Gruen was coming to Baltimore to inspect the design he created for the Hochschild, Kohn Department Store. He decided to set up a meeting with Gruen. Jim was excited. The master was coming."

Daniels continued his description of the meeting between Rouse and Gruen: "Our star features were the placement of the palm trees and a small fountain that spit out water, and a bird cage with cockatoos that crapped over everything. Jim asked me to wait on the balcony at the opposite end for him and Gruen. From there you could see the full length of the concourse. So here comes Jim and Victor, a man about five feet in stature. With an FDR cigarette holder clamped in his mouth, Gruen strutted along, Jim describing his new concept.

"It wasn't the prettiest of malls, but we were very proud of it. Jim then began gesturing with large sweeps of his arms. Finally they arrived on the balcony with me and Victor apparently hadn't yet said a word. And when Jim couldn't stand it any longer, he turned to Gruen and again stretching out his arms to accommodate the scene before him asked, 'Well Victor, what do you think?' Outspoken as he was, Gruen didn't hesitate: 'Jeemy, it's atrocious!' He was particularly overwhelmed with the indoor trees in our palm court. 'How will people see the merchandise?'"

Jim and Bill Rouse initially had difficulty filling the stores in Harundale when it opened October 1, 1958. Years later, a front-page story in the *Wall Street Journal* still stated "a grave foreboding for Harundale." But the reporter was wrong. Harundale *was* profitable. Most architects in this period clung to freestanding cookie-cutter stores and retailers felt safer in renting space in those surroundings. But the next year, Towson Plaza (now owned by The Rouse Company) opened as an enclosed center with "41 fine stores and parking for 3,000 cars." The enclosed mall was here to stay and James W. Rouse & Company and CRD were in a leadership position to capitalize on that fact. By mid-year 1960, the company had grown to one hundred and thirty employees.

Among the new hires was W. Boulton "Bo" Kelly, an old-line Baltimorean who got his education at Gilman, Princeton and the Marine Corps. Upon discharge, the father of four entered Harvard Graduate School of Design. It was during his summer break when he was interviewed for the Rouse position. He was asked to visit Jim and Libby's home on Overlook Lane in North Baltimore. "When I got there, ready to make my best presentation," said Kelly, "I had to confront Jim doing his exercises standing on one of those balance beams with a metal cylinder under it. You can imagine how disconcerting that is, talking about yourself while your audience is trying to keep from touching the floor or worse, falling. I mean it was awful." Apparently it was one of Rouse's idiosyncrasies to lay open an otherwise confident job applicant. Once when Jim was interviewing a prospective secretary, he fiddled with a long Venetian blind cord as he explained the rudiments of the job. Speaking softly, he began to weave the cord through the arms of his chair, then drawer handles and back to the chair interlacing himself into an ornate web. Unable to concentrate, the woman got up and fled.

Bo Kelly was able to handle the apparently planned distractions. He was hired and met others of the Rouseketeers, as they playfully called themselves at headquarters on West Saratoga Street. "As I recall," said Bo, "when I arrived in the office Jim was in the middle of putting together one of those Scandinavian fold-boats to be used as an employee goodwill builder. It had to be assembled from sticks and rubberized canvas that were spread over the floor. Jim showed his lack of hand skills. An hour later, after the rest of the staff had gone back to work, he finally called in an expert to finish the boat. As I circulated around the offices, Jim's secretary showed me a scrapbook of employee photographs. 'Now you're about to become part of our family,' she said. It suddenly occurred to me that I may be joining a cult," he laughed.

By now Jim was traveling with a heady crowd. Besides celebrities and the powerful, he sought out creative people wherever he went. "He had met Walt Disney, the builder of animated films and Disneylands, and Joyce Hall, who headed Hallmark Greeting Cards," Ned Daniels continued. "The three of them used to get together once a year and just create. Joyce Hall particularly was captivated with Jim Rouse's ability to use his eyes and talents. Jim worshipped Disney because he felt he had great imagination and attention to detail. He would say, 'You can walk through one of his projects and there isn't a piece of paper or cigarette butt anywhere. It was beautifully maintained.'"

Rouse also noted in a later speech at Harvard University, "I hold a view that the greatest piece of urban design in the United States today is Disneyland. It fulfills all the functions it set out to accomplish, unself-consciously, usefully and profitably to its owners and developers. I find more to learn in the standards that have been set and in the goals that have been achieved…than in any other single piece of physical development in the country."

Harvard took the speech fairly lightly. Said one attendee: "Shopping centers are issues you deal with, but it's not something that's really important to the total idea of urban design." But before his speech, brother Bill took to the stage to introduce his younger sibling. He went on and on and told how he put Jim through school and inferred he was the man behind the man. To Jim listening from the wing, it was a terrible gaff, a put-down by his own brother before such a prestigious audience. He was livid. He wanted to go out and throttle Bill and had to be held back. Besides the humiliation, there was all that time, money and effort he had put into the preparation.

"Jim tried to do a project with Disney," said Daniels. The two conferred in Jim's office in Cross Keys. "Walt had just started the Environmental Prototype City of Tomorrow (EPCOT), but the work was just too complicated for Rouse at that time. I'm not sure we wouldn't have been swallowed up by the deal, but it became much too involved and we backed off. I think both parties were relieved that we did. It was so much based on Jim and Walt's admiration for each other. The structures of the two companies were so different," said Daniels.

Interestingly, there were some in the company who thought Jim looked like the Disney cartoon character, Jiminy Cricket, and, behind his back, some referred to him as Jiminy. Had good-natured Jim Rouse heard about the comparison to that cute enchanting figure, he probably would have chuckled.

"And in 1960," continued Daniels, "we were in the process of developing the six hundred thousand square feet of retail space at Cherry Hill near Philadelphia, which took us from the minor to major leagues. In addition, there was Charlottetown, North Star Mall in San Antonio, Texas, and we were exploring retail projects in Cincinnati, Pittsburgh and Louisville. And The Village of Cross Keys was about to appear on the horizon."

At a meeting of the Rouse board of directors, a number of projects were discussed, the shopping centers in progress, the mortgage business and a golf course owned by the Baltimore Country Club that had been lingering in negotiations for more than a year. The only things that were holding up the purchase was its location and the cost. Rouse learned that the property had been partially condemned by the city in 1958 for construction purposes. Then on January 14, 1960, Baltimore City bought the southern-most 37.5 acres of the golf course for the Jones Falls Expressway and sites for two new high schools. The dimensions of the links were reduced to such an extent that the club decided to abandon it and dispose of the remaining northern parcel as best it could, commensurate with the wishes of club members and the adjacent Roland Park residential community.

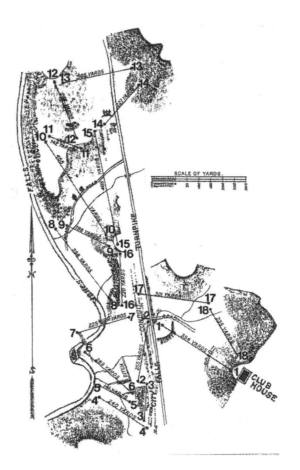

This is a layout of the Roland Park Golf Course when it was proposed in 1897. It is the land on which The Village of Cross Keys was built. The 10th green and 11th tee were moved to the west side of Falls Road so golfers wouldn't have to shoot across the road. Only the 17th tee required a golf shot over the road. A few trolley cars were hit accidentally or on purpose.—Enoch Pratt Library

The Baltimore Country Club was first established in 1897 as the Roland Park Golf Club, but Maryland's first 18-hole course was to be short lived. By 1917, seeds of discontent had been growing among club members over Baltimore City's planned extension of its boundary north into Baltimore County and taking in Roland Park (Annexation Act of 1918 gave fifty square miles more to the city) with subsequently higher taxes. Creation of a second golf course in a suburban location was discussed. Contributing to members' dissatisfaction was the periodic overflowing of the Jones Falls, which dumped silt on several holes, and the danger to golfers crossing the Jones Falls Pike, which was becoming more heavily traveled by trolleys and automobiles.

To replace the golf course, the country club board considered sites in Greenspring Valley, between Rockland and Ruxton, and even Gibson Island, which was offered by club member Stuart Symington who owned the Chesapeake island. On September 12, 1926, the club opened its new twin 18-hole courses known as Five Farms, off Jenifer Road in Baltimore County.

In 1961, Baltimore Country Club was offering the northern sixty-eight acres of its lower golf course along the west side of Falls Road at $25,000 an acre. The cost was hotly debated by the CRD board members, but approval was finally given for Jim to continue negotiations. He again contacted the club and expressed his interest, and was told a fast decision was called for because there were now several other parties, at least one of which was an excellent prospect to buy. While the board thought the cost was too rich, two days later on June 16, 1961, CRD closed the $1.7 million deal.

Jim Rouse was back and forth to his first up-scale enclosed shopping mall, Cherry Hill, in southern New Jersey. This time he had hired designer Victor Gruen. It had grand courts, kiosks and open public spaces such as had never been seen before, fountains, tropical landscaping, vast skylights, living birds and inviting open store fronts. With its first phase completed October 11, 1961, Cherry Hill with its seventy-five stores "marked the company's coming of age." It was the building of successive shopping centers that occupied much of the company for the better part of the 1960s. By the end of the decade, there were seventeen Rouse shopping centers and five more under construction. Rouse was first to learn that marketplaces needed large volumes of retail business to be successful—in some instances from ten to twelve million visitors annually.

"We woke up one Friday morning and Jim Rouse had bought this sixty-eight-acre piece of a golf course from the Baltimore Country Club and immediately started to prepare a plan of how we were to develop it," said Daniels. As he tossed his butane lighter on top of a sheath of papers resting on an umbrella-table in the brightly lit courtyard of the Cross Keys Village Square, he began describing the creation of The Village of Cross Keys. In a very real sense, Daniels knew more about the urban development than even Jim Rouse who devoted only six pages to it in his lengthy autobiography.

In his letter transmitting the contract to the Baltimore Country Club, Jim Rouse wrote: "It will be our purpose to plan one of the truly great apartment communities in the country." Further, his new village would be modeled on European garden cities and the historically successful Roland Park.

Once the land was acquired, all of the CRD talent and imagination was brought to bear on the development of what was called "a suburban-like community within the city." The tract was in a location most developers today would covet. Yet in those days, there were few who could meet the tough qualifications set by the Baltimore Country Club and its Roland Park residents, but Jim Rouse felt he was the person to tackle the demanding task.

After the purchase, came more negotiations with the club's board of governors. They authorized an independent architectural and planning committee to oversee the project and make certain that many agreed-upon criteria were met. On the board were Charles H. Buck, chairman; Charles M. Nes, an architect; Bernard M. Willemain, a planner; Gustav J. Requardt, an engineer; and Archibald C. Rogers, another architect. Also recorded in the deed was the stipulation that every step of development was to be reviewed by the board, and at times, with members of the Roland Park community. As an example, on December 22, 1961, The Roland Park Civic League Zoning Committee, headed by its chairman Charles T. Turner sent a rather heavy-handed letter to James W. Rouse & Co., Inc., with the salutation: "Gentleman." After Turner reviewed some of the details of his committee, he wrote: "As you know, the Roland Park Civic League is vitally interested in maintaining the existing zoning throughout its area and in the past has vehemently opposed and successfully fought every attempt at rezoning in the Roland Park area." Then the League's president, Edward A. Supplee, held a special meeting of residents from the east side of Falls Road, the Park's neighborhood immediately adjacent to the proposed new community.

The meeting was held at the country club. Jim and his colleagues showed up with two versions of what could be built on the site "across the road." The first panel of graphics set on the easel showed an illustration of barracks-like structures covering a flattened golf course. It was created to meet all the zoning requirements of the basic agreement, but was woefully unimaginable. The audience stretched forward, some with wrinkled noses, others giving audible groans. The second panel showed attractive open spaces, a lake, varying designs of townhomes, mid- and high-rise apartments and a commercial shopping area, all sensitive to the natural curves of the countryside and the trees. But in the second concept, Bill Rouse explained the property would have to be rezoned to accommodate the density and commercial aspects of the second plan. Over ninety percent of the property owners attending approved the second plan even though it called for rezoning.

Jim never met with a big group. He'd pick weeknights and meet with residents on this road or that road, vestrymen of some church or other. He never spoke with more than ten or twelve persons. "In small groups, you can rationalize understanding and response," he said. "If you have a group of fifty or sixty, there always will be someone who will stand up and shout and put the whole meeting in disarray. It only takes one or two to turn the whole group against you." Cross Keys was the prototype for strategies used in the development of Columbia.

By now, Jim Rouse was well recognized by the Baltimore business community. He was a founding member of the Greater Baltimore Committee and was invited to sit on councils, lecture before prestigious groups and provide ideas for struggling cities. His interest in urban housing for the poor was drawing national attention. Many of his successful shopping centers were being strung across the nation. U. S. presidents began to seek his counsel.

No one is sure what made him the genius he was. Ned Daniels was with the Rouse Company during its years of dynamic growth. He agreed that Jim was indeed very bright, had a humble "By Golly" warmth that swayed whomever he addressed. But his most valuable quality was being able to identify talent in individuals who could carry out his concepts and plans.

Putting the Cross Keys development team together was an exciting and consuming project for Jim Rouse. On November 22, 1961, he issued a warning to his gathering executives. "We have to pace the work we undertake with the growth of our organization." It was advice that apparently fell on deaf ears, including his own. Ahead lay the most ferocious corporate action ever undertaken by the company requiring highly motivated people.

Ned Daniels described the caliber of persons in the early Rouse organization: "Jerry McDermott was hired from the Red Cross to manage Mondawmin and later managed all our centers. Aubrey Gorman came from BG&E to become vice president of leasing, Skip Cochran came from a bank, Bill Fulton was in legal and Chili Jenkins was development. The six of us ended up being the Rouse development team for the next thirty-two projects."

Having been a friend of Jim's while she was serving as an executive secretary at Fidelity & Deposit, Nancy Allison was asked to become his personal secretary. Through years of taking letters, handling appointments, screening calls and rebuffing aggressive visitors, Miss Allison, a "maiden lady," was totally loyal to her boss. Once when Jim was scurrying around the office carrying a satchel of papers for an appointment, the tattered lining of his madras jacket was hanging out. It was Nancy who followed him around, snip snipping with a scissors to make sure her boss wouldn't embarrass himself. When Jim Rouse retired to Enterprise Foundation, Nancy went with him.

Daniels had been a salesman at Gomprecht & Benesch (a Baltimore home furnishings store), when the magic wand of Rouse touched him. "I think it was his creativity, fair-play and the freedom he gave us that attracted me," said Daniels. "Jim was a charismatic pied piper," he said, "a born leader. His heart was in the right place. He loved people, all kinds of people, especially the poor. Money was secondary to him. Jim would say the most difficult word in the English language is *change*. His whole outlook involved open communities where whites, blacks, Jews, all faiths, and national origins were welcome. That's how we all looked at things then."

In some circles, however, the Rouses might have been called class snobs. Whether this notion was caused by their early exposure to the "what ifs" of their father's business life, or part of their early misfortunes, or part of living on the Eastern Shore where ethnic tolerance is rather low, it may not be known. Integration, now a part of the fabric of America, required some re-thinking for individuals and corporations. One only had to look at the early hierarchy of the Rouse company to see that it was, to a large extent, white Anglo-Saxon Protestant. At the time, one of the few blacks in the company was Walter Powell, a driver, deliveryman and mailroom worker. Jews, like Mort Hoppenfeld, joined the company and were probably kept away from Bill Rouse who could sometimes voice ethnic sentiments. As the company grew, you do get the feeling that Bill made a conscientious effort to curtail prejudice. Much later, he sought out a black secretary. Jack Meyerhoff, a Jewish metropolitan leader, was close to Jim from almost the very beginning and was a major help in getting the company's building operations going, as well as heavily investing in CRD. He was a "founder director" and chairman of the James W. Rouse & Company board.

"I was making $3,500 a year and it took a long time for that to improve," said Ned Daniels. "However, I probably wouldn't have survived anywhere else, so I have no regrets. We were all underpaid. Once when I was in Jim's office—it had to be in the early 60s—George Stillson, by then treasurer of the company, came in and Jim welcomed him back from vacation. 'Where'd you go?' Jim asked smiling. 'I didn't go anywhere,' Stillson muttered. 'You don't pay me enough.'

"That afternoon, Jim went down to the bank and rented a cottage at Rehoboth, Delaware. It became our first corporate vacation home for employees. And through the years I believe there are now about sixty vacation homes along the east coast, from Maine to Florida. At the time, any employee [except married women unless breadwinner], based on seniority and length of service, could be guaranteed a free week in one of them, and under certain circumstances could personally rent a second week," said Daniels. "Jim was always fair. At times, business pressure took him away from his normal concern for individuals. But when he saw inequities, he always tried to correct the situation."

His brother Bill had a different make-up. "At times he could be intolerable," said Bo Kelly. "I was among those who qualified for a couple weeks vacation at Cape Cod. The company rented a row of cottages on a cul-de-sac. Our family had hardly settled in, when Bill Rouse phoned at seven o'clock in the morning to say, 'I'm going to hold a meeting up here.'

Bill was a workaholic, probably a carryover from the insecurity associated with the Great Depression. During his early days as an insurance sales manager, his boss had to force him to take a vacation. And when he returned to work, it was learned that Bill had interviewed fifteen clients and visited five of his salesmen while on his holiday.

"He was quite abrasive," said Kelly. "Once when I was working on some heating and air-conditioning plans for Harundale, Bill was not happy with my report. In fact, he was always unhappy unless his people gave back to him what he considered his own solution to a problem. He had the habit of pulling out a paper-covered sugar cube from his pocket, holding it up and saying, 'You see this? A guy invented a small hole under the paper flap to vent moisture so the wrap wouldn't stick to the sugar.' I guess it was meant to inspire or intimidate us. And he'd forgotten who he told the sugar cube story to, and during later discussions, he'd reach in his pocket and hold up the chunk of sweetness saying, 'You see this?' and the staff would groan.

Jim Rouse was hard at work with his handpicked team of management people and on January 2, 1963, issued a memorandum to centralize responsibility for the development of The Village of Cross Keys. He appointed William E. Finley, a high-powered city planner from Washington, D. C., to take full charge of the project. Leaving nothing to chance, he said Finley would have over-all responsibility to pull together the many details of planning, design, engineering, construction, leasing, promotion and management until Cross Keys was completed. That included handling inquiries from the press, merchants and general public.

As astute as Jim Rouse and his staff were, there was one detail that would eventually leave them breathless. A 4.11 acre piece of land, called the "Spath Tract," was adjacent to the golf course land sold to CRD. Owned by Col. John McC. Mowbray and his investors, it was to become the subject of a lawsuit that worried and saddened Jim Rouse. Mowbray was a life-long employee of The Roland Park Company and its last president when it closed operations in 1959.

He had been a long-time member of the Baltimore Country Club and Jim's personal friend. Mowbray had owned the Spath Tract for many years. His only access to it was through a narrow meandering path in a barren meadow near the golf course over which he drove his car several times a year in order to protect it against eminent domain take-over.

One of the area's landowners in the late 1800s was Anton Spath. He lived in a rambling frame home with elevated grounds supported by a masonry wall in the old Cross Keys Village. Spath, a thrifty German immigrant and a basket maker by trade, slowly amassed a considerable number of properties in the vicinity. One of these was the tract bordering on the Jones Falls creek, on which there was an abundant growth of willow shrubs. From their limber stems, Spath wove baskets for various uses and sold them to his neighbors. Later when Roland Park was being developed, it was reported that the prosperous and aging Spath sold part of his willow grove on the west side of Jones Falls to the Roland Park Company for its sewage disposal field.

It is not known how John Mowbray acquired his portion of the Spath Tract. But as its owner in later years, he decided it was time to make his investment pay off. He and his investors entered into internal deliberations with the Baltimore Country Club to tidy up the sixty-eight acres being sold to Rouse's Community Research and Development. At that point, in exchange for his "meandering path," Mowbray asked the club to trade him a sixty-foot straight road access from Falls Road west to his property near the mid-point of the hundred acres the club was readying for disposition. The trade allowed the club to acquire the dirt path that weaved near a portion of the land recently acquired by CRD. Mowbray and his associate, Sifford Pearre, had already received zoning for a retail shopping center they wanted to build on the tract to take market advantage of the new Cross Keys and the high schools.

But things started to get nasty in the fall of 1962, when Mowbray and Pearre sued the country club *and* Cross Keys in an apparent attempt to get the Spath land and its new sixty-foot road easement rezoned from commercial to *residential* so a high-rise apartment building could be built on it. Jim Rouse was livid and, in court testimony, quickly pointed out the unfair competition it would create for his own up-scale apartments. Further, he noted that the big building would virtually take up the entire lot and give its occupants the advantage of over-looking north onto his beautifully landscaped Village of Cross Keys.

There was a rush by the club and the Mowbray-Pearre group to get the easement exchange completed. Mowbray had an even more cogent reason for speed because the condemnation of the Spath Tract, or whatever portion the city was about to acquire for expressway use, "was quite alive and the court found as a fact that this land would have had little value if it were accessible only by means of the old meandering path. On the other hand, it would suddenly acquire tremendous value if there existed a wide direct right-of-way from Falls Road to the property."

During this interval, there were informal discussions pertaining to the possible acquisition of the Spath Tract by Jim Rouse, no doubt in the expectation that the 4.11 acres would be adaptable for some use in the new Cross Keys planning. An attorney for the Mowbray group suggested that a valuation of $80,000 per acre would be in order although there were earlier attempts to sell the tract to other investors for $60,000 an acre. Rouse was not interested in any such price and evidently saw no reason why his organization should pay more per acre for the rather remote section than it had agreed to pay the club for the sixty-eight acres—$25,000 an acre—an amount initially considered too high by the Rouse board. Jim also testified that he had some investigation made of the Spath Tract and discovered that it was "filled" land and not especially to his liking.

In a stinging one-page letter written to John McC. Mowbray at his Stuart, Florida, home on March 13, 1963, Jim Rouse expressed his displeasure over the turn of events. Blind copies were sent to Franklin Allen, Charles Buck, and directors of CRD and JWR.

The letter started cautiously: "I find it a very unpleasant experience to be at odds with an old friend for whom I have as much respect as I have for you. You may remember our first conversation on the Baltimore Country Club site when we sat together at a Title Guarantee board meeting. You suggested at the time that the Country Club would be particularly interested in a proposal from us as they wanted to sell the land to a developer in whom they had confidence—one who would build a new community in keeping with the character and dignity of Roland Park. I have been very conscious of the special responsibility that this confidence imposed on us, and we have worked earnestly to produce the finest residential community we could conceive. This has cost money, taken time and, inevitably, will introduce a greater risk than moving ahead with a more or less standard apartment project."

In his letter, Rouse further wrote: "Having worked diligently to produce a fine, high quality, low density village community, it is a distressing prospect to see the kind of neighbor which is proposed on the adjacent land.

"You have built an outstanding reputation in Baltimore. Somehow this venture seems unworthy of you, and I am sickened at the prospect of the kind of battle that seems to be ahead to prevent the construction of that which is proposed…"

We are not sure of the impact of the letter, but it shows that Jim Rouse never rolled over whenever he fought for his ideals. Finally, Judge J. Gilbert Prendergast's ruling restricted the Mowbray land to a retail shopping center, and an injunction was issued against a high-rise apartment building. It would appear that the Spath Tract was finally purchased by CRD and eventually became the site of the Cross Keys Quadrangle office campus.

One more trade of land *did* benefit Cross Keys. The city needed eighteen acres along the west bank of the Jones Falls for expressway use. It was owned by the Roland Park Company and contiguous with part of the southwestern edge of the proposed Cross Keys. City officials suggested exchanging a twenty-two acre city-owned easement along the west side of Falls Road (under which lay the city's defunct water conduit) for the eighteen acres, part of which had been Roland Park's sewage processing fields. So the club had to be happy with the transfer. The deal was part and parcel of the sale to CRD and provided the space for the gatehouse and Fallswood I section of Cross Keys along Falls Road.

Just as plans for The Village of Cross Keys got underway, James W. Rouse & Company formed The Howard Research and Development Corporation (HRD). Concurrently, Jim had staff researcher Chili Jenkins create a hypothetical model for a city of a hundred thousand people. It became the basis for Columbia in Howard County. In a fifty-fifty joint venture with Connecticut General Life Insurance Company that ultimately laid out $23.5 million for land, Rouse in the spring of 1963 began purchasing farmland for his planned city. He hired several local real estate brokers who secretly assembled parcels of land, 13,680 acres, in 147 separate deals. It took just nine months and ultimately was the heart of the twenty-two square miles that would become the new town, Columbia, with a projected population of 120,000 (now approaching 96,000).

As early as May 1963, Rouse told his CRD employees at 14 West Saratoga Street that the company would move to new headquarters in the yet-to-be-built Village Square at Cross Keys. "…we are now working with the architects to make [the offices] beautiful, efficient and comfortable for all of us," he wrote in a memo.

As the moment of ground breaking for Cross Keys approached, the new Roland Park relationship with the residents began to change. Some had renewed qualms about the kinds of people the new community would attract and the increased traffic, and their curving roadways being taken over by high-speed newcomers. Rouse promised that Cross Keys streets would not align with those exiting from Roland Park onto Falls Road. Since the Rouse community would be open to all, its covenants dealt only with visual features of Cross Keys. Roland

Park, on the other hand, had the usual covenants dealing with house setbacks and visual aspects, but made racial restrictions part of its "deed and agreement" that covered all separate properties within the development. Clearly, no Jew or Negro was allowed to purchase in Roland Park and Catholics, if known, were discouraged. These ethnic covenants have since been deleted, repudiated and condemned.

Even within the Rouse organization, there were concerns expressed over the type of residents the new Cross Keys would attract. Some worried about the 21209 zip code on which the new village was to be built and Jim Rouse had his staff ask postal authorities to change it to 21210, the prevailing code of Roland Park. Tying into the Roland Park mystique was very important to the marketing success of The Village of Cross Keys. In a very real sense, it would become Roland Park *West*. Today, 21209 includes Mattfeldt-Sabina, the small community just north of the Jones Falls Expressway interchange at Northern Parkway, and 09 continues as it did, but hop-scotches over the new 21210 Cross Keys community, to include Poly-Western high schools and the homes on the east side of Falls Road, just north of Cold Spring.

To extend Cross Keys northward, Rouse tried to buy the adjacent land and fifteen homes perched on the steep service road (old Northern Parkway) that goes up behind Greenfield Nursery at the southwest corner of Falls and the new Northern Parkway. Each property's value was appraised, but the city discouraged the deal when officials thought they might need extra easement in the event Northern Parkway would be enlarged in the future.

One of those properties, the next to last home at the top of the hill, had been the boyhood summer home of H. L. Mencken, the *Sun* columnist who gained fame as a social skeptic and curmudgeon. Baltimore author, Gilbert Sandler, described the era in the 1980 *Quarterly Review of the Mencken Society:* "A remote and beautiful place" Henry would recall of his childhood summer home. For eight years, H. L. and his family lived in the turreted frame home from May through September. South of the house was a farm (now The Village of Cross Keys), where Henry and his young buddies played baseball.

As a youth H. L. Mencken spent his summers in this house overlooking Belvedere Avenue (now Northern Parkway). He played baseball with friends on a farm to the south that today is part of The Village of Cross Keys.

"There was a stretch of wild woodland with banks of morning glories along its path," he later wrote. "Behind the woods was an immense field sloping down towards Baltimore but relatively flat on top. In my day it was a hayfield and we boys used to rent it from the farmer after the hay harvest for use as a baseball field," recalled Mencken. "We paid him $15 a year, well spent." Mencken himself says he played "shortstop, mainly," but that he also pitched. "I was a good base runner but a poor hitter and could not throw as well as the other boys."

7

The Tough Work Begins

Community Research and Development finally made application for The Village of Cross Keys building permit in mid-August 1963. It requested approval "to construct an apartment house at 5100 Falls Road at a cost of $821,000." The first section was already a year behind schedule. The new planned unit development, the largest ever-attempted in Baltimore City, was to include 1,216 apartments and townhouses. The apartments were expected to be located in four nine-story towers containing a total of 600 units. A Village Square shopping center was to be built in two phases: Phase I—35,121 sq. ft. of retail, 39,490 sq. ft. of office and Phase II—28,588 sq. ft. of retail and 38,622 sq. ft. of office and an inn and conference center, restaurant and indoor parking for 880 cars. Estimates for build-out were from three to five years. There was a joke floating around the offices that said, "Land planning was being done by every executive in the Rouse Company and half the people in Roland Park."

As Jim Rouse started staging for his first residential development, he received immeasurable help from around the country. Architect Pietro Belluschi recommended Richard C. Stauffer, a young graduate of M.I.T., to assist in design work. Stauffer and Jim Rouse collaborated on the early site plan for Cross Keys. Taking a page from Frederick Law Olmsted, Jr.'s Roland Park plan, the directive from Rouse was to follow the land contours and not to remove trees except for a few in the footprints of the first section of the $30-million development. Stauffer and Collins-Kronstadt and Associates of Silver Spring, Maryland, designed the first two-story townhomes whose style was called conservative, cozy and contemporary. There was plenty of wood, subtle organic colors, pastel brick and steep rooflines, played against deep roadways, open garages and flower gardens. The trees survived and became a big marketing attraction for these new suburban homes within the city. Eventually Stauffer (and his wife) left the project and became partners in The Store Ltd., managing its new store in Georgetown.

The company was growing so fast, there weren't enough people on board to tackle the increasing problems in building Cross Keys and planning Columbia. Executives were working seventy-hour weeks with Jim leading the way. He could sleep for just a few hours and get up refreshed. There were many times on an airline flight that Jim would fall asleep for five minutes, wake up, and continue working on papers in his lap. There is even the famous story about Jim falling asleep at a stoplight and asking his passenger to wake him when the light turned green. He had probably learned to catnap while working the double shift at the St. Paul Garage and, at the same time, going to law school where he'd snooze just before class. The work load and stresses on individuals and families were sometimes questioned by employees, but never by Jim Rouse. His energy seemed boundless and more stress merely pumped more adrenaline.

Jim always tried to be home for dinner with the family, but after the kids were in bed, out came the briefcase with six inches of material to go over for the next day. His day started at seven. It was Jim's custom to answer typewritten internal memos by writing in a heavy pointed black marker right over the memos sent to him. It was efficient. If a memo brought up a worrisome situation, as often as not, he'd write, "How could this have happen?" in big scrawl across the paper. And he expected an answer. Most Rouse executives got at least five of them during their careers.

On July 1, 1963, Scott Ditch, a patrician graduate of all the best schools, joined the staff of the Rouse company. "The company had never done anything remotely like Cross Keys before," recalled Ditch. "They were completely unaware of how to go about marketing it. I guess that was one of the reasons why they brought me on board."

Ditch had experience with Vansant Dugdale & Co., a Baltimore advertising agency. Then he left and took a position with the *County Newsweek,* a Towson newspaper, as its editor. One morning in mid-summer of 1963, he got the word from owner Fenwick Keyser that he was selling out to the *Jeffersonian,* another county paper. "I was told they wouldn't need two editors," said Ditch, "so my head was on the block." Keyser, who knew Jim Rouse's brother Bill, introduced Ditch to him. "Bill asked me, 'What can you do for us?' I told him I was a newspaper editor, before that I was in advertising and before that served many years flying combat in the Marine Corps. Bill said, 'I'd like you to meet my brother, Jim.'

Top left, clockwise: *Scott Ditch, a former newspaper editor and advertising executive was hired by Rouse when it became apparent that the new Village of Cross Keys apartments would not sell themselves. He was then assigned to the new town of Columbia, Maryland.*
Frank O. Gehry opened an office on Roland Avenue to design buildings in Cross Keys and Columbia. He is considered the greatest living architect in the world today.—Gehry Partners
Monk Askew was one of Rouse's in-house architectural designers for many years. He continues to work for the company as a consultant.

"Bill asked me to bring some samples of my work to his Ridgewood Road home in Roland Park. He didn't want to meet in his office. I didn't realize all this stuff [Columbia] was very hush-hush. When I got there he and Jim Rouse anxiously asked to see my work. I opened a portfolio of news clips and advertising tear sheets and as I flipped through them, Jim stopped me and said, 'What about that?' He was pointing to a full-page feature I had written about a strange community built by Henry Drushel Perky, an entrepreneur, explorer, lawyer, teacher and inventor of Shredded Wheat. In 1903, Perky decided he was going to build a whole new town from scratch in Baltimore County. He acquired four thousand acres on the edge of *My Lady's Manor* near what is now Oldfield School. When Jim Rouse saw that story on Henry Perky who sixty years before had held concepts similar to those he planned for Columbia, he was taken aback.

Perky's town was to be called The Republic of Oread (pronounced OR-e-add) and its motto was "Learn to Do by Doing." Resident students would raise crops and preserve them, as well as supply milk to Baltimore city. These would be Oread's main businesses. Perky's plan was to build industries and residential homes, a meeting hall and trolleys and trains to service Oread. But then financial problems struck Perky and his new town. He wired potential investors around the country and pleaded for help. Finally investors started to rally. Someone took the good news up to his house. But they found the tireless visionary in his bathtub, dead. Depressed, he had taken his own life.

That one story may have won the job for Ditch. "Jim and Bill had been interviewing me to be on the Columbia team, but they couldn't tell me" said Ditch. "I didn't know the purpose for which I was hired, but later was told I would be the communicator with Howard County. To get my feet wet with the company, I was assigned to The Village of Cross Keys."

Jim Rouse and his chief planner, Mort Hoppenfeld, took a six-week trip to Europe in the late summer of 1963 to study examples of new and old towns and villages. They discovered the charm of garden cities in England and the Scandinavian countries, particularly Tapiola near Helsinki, Finland, some of whose features would be folded into The Village of Cross Keys, as well as other future residential, commercial and office communities. Hoppenfeld had joined the company as Bill Finley's deputy and was a leading architect, planner and academic. Jim got much of his early design direction from Mort. "The two probably laid out most of the roads in Cross Keys," said Rich Altman, a Rouse land planner.

The earthmovers and bulldozers rumbled onto the land of Cross Keys in September 1963. The area was changing. Ten months earlier, the cutting, filling, setting piers and paving for the new Jones Falls Expressway (I-83) was completed and state, county and city officials cut the ribbon to open the six-lane highway, first conceived a decade earlier. The southern portion of the golf course tract, together with other nearby acreage, had been the repository for excess land from some of the expressway cuts. The fill dirt became the Poly-Western athletic field covering one of the city's smoldering dumpsites. The area along Coldspring west became a ramp for the northbound lanes of the expressway. Also buried among the works of the expressway was the old Hamilton Mill dam and millrace that used to cut wood veneer on the east bank of the Jones Falls below where Harper House now stands. In 1832, brothers Robert and James Hamilton, Jr., Scottish immigrants living in Mt. Washington, bought the site to build custom furniture made with rosewood and mahogany veneers.

Forgotten, too, was Camp Small, a tiny bivouac of Union Zouave soldiers from York who in 1862 were tented on the west bank of Jones Falls at Melville, just across the stream near the vinegar factory. They guarded five miles of the Northern Central Railroad (Woodberry to Relay House at Lake Roland) from Confederate raids to burn bridges, tear up tracks, destroy telegraph lines, and steal horses and supplies. A year before, following the Civil War's "first blood" between citizens and Massachusetts troops on Pratt Street in Baltimore, April 19, 1861, Mayor George W. Brown had directed police and Maryland National Guard troops to destroy many of those same bridges and tracks from Baltimore to Cockeysville to prevent northern forces from again coming into the city.

Ironically, just over the eastern ridge in the Stony Run basin of Roland Park were encamped Confederate cavalrymen from Fort Myer, Virginia. Another bit of irony, in 1863, both Hiram Woods, owner of some early Roland Park acreage and William McDonald, builder of the "Guilford" mansion, both were arrested for appearing to signal nearby Confederate soldiers from their upstairs' windows. McDonald was imprisoned in Ft. McHenry and died soon after his release.

The first public announcement of the new town of Columbia came in October 1963. "It was like adding the proverbial eight-hundred pound gorilla to the company's workday," said Scott Ditch. "Here comes this tremendous project with the same people from Cross Keys doing the work. Jim told the Howard County commissioners that he'd be back in a year with a full plan. The first development director of Cross Keys was Bill Finley, but he was also development director of Columbia. It took a huge amount of Jim Rouse, Mort Hoppenfeld and the rest of the team, shifting between the two communities. It had a major impact on the pace at Cross Keys. Rouse had expected things to go smoothly, but they didn't. It certainly slowed things down." At that moment in time, The Village of Cross Keys became a stepchild.

On top of this chaotic setting, President John Kennedy was assassinated on November 23, 1963. It was against this demoralizing background that the first Cross Keys townhomes were being built.

Back home from his research trip to Europe, Rouse encouraged his staff to visit shopping and residential communities around the country. He wanted tips on styles, merchant mix and rent structures. Walter Durham, a consultant to the company, recommended that the Cross Keys development "stay close to nature." He suggested using vines, lots of arbors, trellises, lattices and espaliering along with general landscaping ideas that Jim passed on to his sister, Dia. She and her husband, C. O'Donnell Pascault, had been in the real estate business in Chicago and Easton. Both would join the Rouse Company. Dia was an ambitious woman with an instinctive feeling for residential landscaping. She is credited with creating most of the award-winning shrub and flower layouts in the village, particularly at the south and north ends and in the courtyard of Village Square. She was a hard-charger—called a "tiger" and a "bird" by those who worked with her.

Jim also was taken by Durham's suggestion that each hamlet should have something of its own character. "I am amazed at how graciously and how humanly he has caught the spirit that people would love to have in a residential community," he said. Libby Rouse also thought the open backyards and intimacy would generate a friendliness seldom achieved in an urban neighborhood.

Richard Altman remembers those early days when he was a full-time employee of James Rouse & Company and later a consultant. His specialty at the company was land planning and design. He recalls "the first phase of Cross Keys Village was designed by Jim, Mort Hoppenfeld and Dia Pascault. Also, Ned Daniels and, to some degree, Bob Tennenbaum and Dick Stauffer."

At the outset, there was newspaper publicity, but little paid advertising. The model townhomes at 14, 16 and 18 Hamlet Hill Road were up and opened in February 1964. At first, all units at Cross Keys were to be rented with the first ninety-eight townhomes in the "Greens," (Palmer, Olmsted and Bouton) coming online in March. However, the development was not attracting enough attention from prospective buyers. Stern memos came out of the Rouse office criticizing the early ads and asking why more wasn't being done to market the apartments. Jim Rouse may even have offered some silent prayers.

He was a religious man, and Libby had a tremendous spiritual influence on him. Her discussions of what kind of community would make a homemaker's life easier helped catalyze Jim's thoughts about Cross Keys and Columbia. Jim was a solid, well-rounded person—even used mild profanity at times—but he was religious, deeply religious. One of his concepts for Cross Keys was to have a nondenominational chapel. Although mentioned by him in letters and an annual report, few staffers remember this proposed feature. It might have been Libby Rouse who suggested "doing things in your business to allow people to have the opportunity to worship."

Many concerts were given in the courtyard of The Village Square. The shelter at the rear was once thought to be Rouse's nondenominational chapel. It was thus used in an Easter "sunrise service" during the early years of the village.——R.R. Rodney Boyce

While Libby doesn't specifically remember her husband's interest, Jim's idea for a chapel in Cross Keys may have been manifested in other ways. Some believe the large meeting room in the hotel was meant to double as a place for interfaith worship, or perhaps the small wooden outdoor shelter in the Village Square where the community's first Easter "sunrise service" was held. It was designer Betty Cooke who remembered "a low all-purpose building had been designed and was to be built as a house of worship on the western edge of a planned lake that would have encompassed the present parking lot between the tennis barn and the hotel," she said. "They even built a model of it."

Too much time had elapsed without meeting rent goals in Cross Keys and Scott Ditch had to speak up. "I had a discussion which rolled into an argument with Bill Rouse and Bill Winstead, who was working Cross Keys sales at the time. I said we would *have* to advertise to sell the townhomes. 'Oh no,' said Bill Rouse, 'it'll draw the wrong kind of people and we don't want that.' They had hoped the homes would sell by word of mouth."

It didn't happen, and things were getting very touchy among the top echelon. In an unusually brutal and sarcastic reference to their early advertising, Jim told his older brother in a four-page memo that "two advertisements that appeared in Sunday's newspaper did not receive all the careful attention that such an ad, under most circumstances, should and would have received. However, while understanding this," he wrote, "I must also acknowledge that the ads were a sharp disappointment." He noted the poor position of the ads and that the main selling feature was "15 minutes to downtown."

"First of all, it is 10 minutes to downtown from Cross Keys. Secondly, nowhere in this ad…does it ever say that we have apartments for rent. If I had to pick that feature of Cross Keys that did least to emphasize our major advantages, it would have been our proximity to downtown…. Why in the world would we try to make this our most outstanding feature? In neither ad," he went on, "it seemed to me, did we get across our environment or our advantages. The consecutive listing of features was dull and weak. Neither the format nor the copy carried in its appearance and style, an atmosphere of distinction. The map was exceedingly bad, failing even to achieve its main purpose of making us look convenient. Worst of all was the corny phrase 'a gracious address.' This is the standard badge of people trying to make a high income, snob appeal, when they really don't have it."

Finally, Jim's memo issued on Tuesday concluded with a near-impossible request: "I assume that this was a rush, and that an advertising program is being devised, and will be underway by not later than next Sunday." Deadline for Sunday newspaper display advertisements was Friday at noon and certain special sections had to be ordered six-weeks in advance.

Even as late as 1964, insecurity crept into the mind of Jim Rouse. He desperately wanted Cross Keys to be successful. Jim was, by his own admission, so scared of failure that he could not bring himself to therapeutically share his misgivings with his closest associates. "We must realize that we are real amateurs in this field," he wrote to his brother in September. "Whatever our professional capacities may be in shopping centers, we have never built, promoted, and successfully leased an apartment project. Thus, as in our early days at Mondawmin, we must look, listen, and learn from all sources that can contribute as we gradually master this task. To this end it would seem essential that both you and Ned (and perhaps others) should visit and carefully note the merchandising and advertising policies of every apartment project in the Baltimore area that is remotely in competition with us.... We should also be continuously trying to find out what the leasing record is in...Elkridge Estates, Highfield House, Ruxton Towers, 3900 N. Charles, Belvedere Towers, etc."

The idea of exclusivity in leasing was Jim's alone. In an earlier memo to Bill, and carboned to other team members, he said, "I think it is VERY IMPORTANT that we really not accept an application from anyone outside of the Roland Park community and the Baltimore Country Club until the priority date (November 1, 1964) is expired. The main point of all this is that the quieter we can keep our leasing program in the early stages—the less attention it attracts—the better off we will be. If we could possibly manage to lease all or most of the original 98 units before any kind of a public offering or public attention to the project, we would have gone a long way toward establishing the ultimate atmosphere of the Village."

He was sure that Roland Parkers and club members would be waiting in line to rent the new homes. But even after a lavish public relations booklet "Reflections on Roland Park" had been thoughtfully researched and written by Laverne Finley, printed by the company and distributed throughout Roland Park, it generated few leasing inquiries. Prospects turned grim. Some thought Jim's idea was too elitist, perhaps even racist. There was concern for how the black population might react. Already there were plans to assure that a good cross section of the population was included in the community especially as "the less expensive garden apartments" became available.

The leasing of the ninety-eight townhouse apartments was nearly six months behind schedule. During the summer months leasing had been on a selective basis attracting only twelve rented apartments. Some blame could be placed on the tardiness of the completion of the gatehouse, pool, tennis court and clubhouse. The public didn't have the ability to visualize the other components of the property and leasing remained flat into the fall.

Coming out of one meeting of company executives, there were head scratchings and ashen faces. Despite all the concern over lagging leases, it was learned that applicants for the homes would have to make appointments for inspections and there would be no "open houses." The concept was contrary to all real estate marketing strategies.

At the same time as the marketing at Cross Keys was floundering, there were hundreds of meetings dealing with Columbia and everyone was trying to tell *something* without telling *anything* until the whole project was in place. "We didn't want a lot of controversy," said Scott Ditch. "Then once the new town plan was presented and approved, we had to go for zoning in November of 1964.

There was a big deficiency of staff at a time when we had to build lakes, create roads and put in utilities." When Finley was pulled off Cross Keys to Columbia, Ned Daniels took over as project manager.

In July 1965, James W. Rouse & Company and CRD moved into 40,000 square feet of new executive offices in the first section of the Village Square. Mortgage servicing and data processing remained at 14 West Saratoga. A year later, CRD became the dominant corporation, but the James W. Rouse & Company division continued to grow operating mortgage banking offices in Baltimore, Chicago, Pittsburgh, San Francisco, in addition to its early office opened in the District of Columbia.

"Unknown to anyone in the company," said Scott Ditch, "I had worked up an advertisement—designed and written—which was on the floor behind my desk. One day I got a call from Jim Rouse saying we'd been at this marketing too long now. The first ninety-eight houses had been completed and a year later they had only rented, I think, eighteen of them. I told Jim I had taken a shot at something he might like and he asked me to bring it to his office. 'My gosh!' Jim exclaimed his approval of the full-page ad before him. 'Where would you run it?'"

Ditch had the entire plan in his mind: "I suggested we insert ads in the rotogravure section of the *Sunday Sun*. No one had ever tried to sell real estate in that part of the newspaper before. Jim listened as I explained the demographics and cost and he said, Run it on Sunday. I had to tell him that the closing date was six-weeks in advance. With Jim's enthusiasm running particularly high, we did schedule it and it did work. Things started to take hold, but then the pressure was on. We had to produce an ad every week. Ned Daniels and I did most of the work. He got his wife Sydney to pose for one of the ads; I got my wife Sue for one, and staff members for others. Mort Tadder did the photography and Joel Adler the art direction and design. We had all kinds of good fun doing the ads and six months later eighty-five of the townhomes had been leased with the first occupants moving in during spring of 1964. And it also was interesting that the people who were renting were top of the line, in their fields and professions."

"In Cross Keys, we felt reasonably in control as we moved into the first phase of development," said Ned Daniels. "With the gatehouse completed, we decided to open an art gallery in its public rooms as part of the grand opening marketing effort. Our first ad was a photograph of the gatehouse with the headline 'The Art of Welcome.' It was created by Scott Ditch to convey that this was truly a special place. Called the Gatehouse Gallery, it was a beautifully lit space and had moveable panels. *The Sun* newspaper even covered it with a full-page news article. The first exhibit was on owls. There must have been fifty or sixty prints, paintings, sculptures and artifacts. We did about three shows—they were really good—then we needed the space for more offices and that ended the gallery."

The Cross Keys gatehouse was first used as an art gallery, then a sales office. All telephone services and security emanate from this building.

As the first neighborhood of Bryant Woods in Columbia was being built, crews also were scrambling to translate architect Frank O. Gehry's design into the 20,000 sq. ft. Exhibition Center. The day before it was to open June 21, 1967, Dia Pascault told the landscaping company to re-lay the sod and replant some of the shrubbery. (In the summer of 2001, The Rouse Company announced that it would tear down the Exhibit Center in Columbia. A preservation group in Howard County included the 34-year-old Exhibit Center on a "Top 10 Endangered Sites List." Gehry couldn't be reached for comment about the planned demolition, but two of his collaborating architects who worked on the project, N. David O'Malley and C. Gregory Walsh "said they would not mind if the Center was torn down." O'Malley added: "At the time this was designed, we were also doing Kay's jewelry stores and gas stations in Irvine.")

"The first completed hamlets in Cross Keys were Bouton Green, Olmsted Green and Palmer Green," said Daniels. These names and others were selected by Jim Rouse for streets, buildings and meeting rooms in Cross Keys. They were based on notables who planned and built Roland Park and a few contemporaries who had personally helped him. They included Edward H. Bouton, Frederick Law Olmsted, Edward L. Palmer, Jr., Robert J. W. Hamill, Willi Dunn, Robert Goodloe Harper (spelled Goodlow at Cross Keys) and Guy T. O. Hollyday and others. He also felt the names would appeal to his neighbors in Roland Park because Bouton, developer of Roland Park, had asked the Olmsteds in 1902 to compile a list of names for streets, most of which had an English ring to them or had some reference to trees and plants. They intentionally used the term "road" instead of "street" because it sounded more naturalistic. In many ways, the detail-oriented, high-energy Bouton was the twin of Jim Rouse.

Ned Daniels said Jim Rouse had visited Canada and seen some interesting architectural work at a college in Toronto. It had an atmosphere that Jim found intriguing. And after some meetings and negotiations, the architectural firm of Murray and Fleiss, also of that city, agreed to come to Baltimore and design the first phase of the retail area, Village Square, which ended at the enclosed bridge where the original flower shop kiosk had been located. Jim Murray was the partner in charge.

The word was getting out in the mid-1960s. Owners of small retail shops and entrepreneurs started calling and negotiating for space in Village Square. Daniels had known about Octavia Dugan. "She was helping her cousin with a dress shop on Cold Spring Lane," he said. "We talked her into opening a tiny shop in the southeast corner. She was enormously successful because it was a dress shop that catered to chic women, not avant-garde, but polite women's good-looking clothes. It appealed to the ladies of Roland Park. Then we found a cheese merchant, a men's tweed shop and right next to the north stairway, we started The Roost Restaurant.

"The original Roost was owned by James W. Rouse & Company," revealed Daniels. "When we had difficulty finding an unusual eating place to bring in, Ed Dann of our design staff and I put the restaurant together. I went to galleries here and in Philadelphia for artwork and charged it to the company. We had a collection of 250 original etchings, paintings and sculptures—all the art was of birds—all kinds, including chickens. We hired a manager and the restaurant became a very nice place to eat and be seen." Several years later, The Roost became part of the hotel. And it became even more popular as a coffee shop. Its breakfasts were known as *"power breakfasts"* and everyone who was anybody wanted to be seen there in the morning. Often attending were the mayor, governor, clergy, council members, corporate CEOs, the non-profits, everyone nodding, shaking hands and whispering the yet-to-be-disclosed news of the day. It was marvelous. There are still vestiges of the original Roost in the dining room and lobby of the current Radisson Hotel. "I just saw one of the roosters in the Cross Roads Restaurant that was in our original collection," said Daniels. "I should also add that Ed Dann designed the hand-made cast-aluminum street lamps for Cross Keys, as well as the park benches.

"The early tenants in Phase I of the Village Square were mostly new entrepreneurs," he continued. "The grocery store, barber shop, bakery and, of course, The Store Ltd. Sally Jones had sort of a gift shop before going to women's clothing. There used to be a walk-through from the east courtyard to the parking lot and our leasing office was on the corner between where Talbots is now and the former La Perfumerie. We had a bank—Equitable Trust—that provided some of our construction loans. Its president, John Luetkemeyer, lived in Roland Mews." A list of Village Square retail tenants can be found in the Appendix.

There were so many quality touches when Cross Keys first opened. For instance, each retail store had its own symbol hanging over the front of its facade. The Roost had a chicken shape, the pharmacy, a mortar and pestle, and Octavia had her name outlined on a filigree rectangle. There must have been fifty of these heavy, handcrafted steel and wood signs. Twenty years ago, their uniqueness attracted the eye of Trixie Rumford, curator of the Abby Aldrich Rockefeller Folk Art Collection in Williamsburg, Virginia. She was doing her graduate work in American craft art. Trixie took Polaroids of each of the signs, but she couldn't remember what happened to the photographs that would have been a nice addition beyond the one shown in this book. Further complimenting the work, she said: "I do remember thinking at the time, it was the finest collection of contemporary generic signage in America."

The filigree sign over this shop was once an attraction for each retailer in the Village Square. Some of the signs are in storage waiting for new shops to utilize them.

"I can remember standing out near the courtyard bridge one evening," said Ned Daniels. "There was a bright, colorful paneled wall with all kinds of interestingly shaped viewing holes designed and painted by Betty Cooke and Bill Steinmetz. People could watch work on Phase II expansion where the inn and other shops were being erected. It was usually a muddy pit with all kinds of construction equipment and materials standing around. Trash blew through like it was a wind tunnel. Looking around I thought, my gosh, do we know what we're doing? I admit there were doubts.

"John Luetkemeyer came walking through one day and said to me, 'I visit here every once in a while and I can't imagine why we're building a branch bank here except for Jim Rouse.'" Daniels replied, "Mr. Luetkemeyer, I'm here to get the place built and I think you'll find it will be a different atmosphere once it's complete. Ultimately, the Cross Keys location became one of Equitable Bank's most successful."

A bank robber must have sensed the growing deposits. He drove up to the south entrance where Talbots is now located and parked, ran in the bank and made his announcement. In the meantime, a woman had driven up and parked behind him as was the custom in those days, "just to make a quick deposit." Of course when the robber ran out, he couldn't move his car. He may have surrendered in frustration.

"I guess the point I'm making is this," said Daniels. "In those days, with Jim Rouse at the midway point of building Cross Keys, his personal philosophy was 'go for it.' He exuded confidence. He had this reputation for imagination, doing things that never had been done before. Try things, fall on your face, get up and try again. He had enormous respect for himself. He may have looked like he just came out of a Goodwill carry-on shop—worn and tattered clothes, stained sweatband on his porkpie hat, madras coat buttoned at the wrong button, the lining hanging out—it was a disaster, but with his imagination and creativity, we'd follow him anywhere," said Daniels.

During those first years of Cross Keys development, there were other problems. Capital became scarce and cash flow had to be increased. It was a roller coaster ride. Interest rates were soaring and occupant complaints were close behind. Jim Rouse and his executive committee worked tirelessly to get a handle on the blossoming project. Everyone agreed, if the development was to survive, more cash would have to be generated. It was decided that Cross Keys would have to go "condominium" and allow the renters and the public to *buy* the homes. But it would take time and lawyers to prepare the mortgage documents. In the meantime, there was a reordering of internal policies and a tightening of resources. It was proposed that even the golf course fairway sod be sold to the new Memorial Stadium on 33rd Street and the eight greens to the city links. The greens on the east side of Falls Road were still to be used by the country club for chip and putt.

In the final phase of construction of the Village Square, Rouse was ready to build the Cross Keys Inn, pool and underground parking, adding two stories and 55,000 square feet. The expansion had been designed by architect Jim Murray. A permanent mortgage of $2.4 million was secured together with a construction loan. Rouse said the work would be completed by July 1965. The first of three elevator apartment buildings also got underway. Helping to clean up the southern end of Cross Keys, the Poly-Western High Schools were completed and had opened a year earlier.

At a meeting of stockholders, October 31, 1965, Ned Daniels was singled out by Jim Rouse. "There is a special vice president in this division [Commercial Development] whom I frequently described as the conscience of our company. He is Ned Daniels—whose experience and 'feel' over a wide spectrum of functions we have to perform—planning, design, tenant performance, property man-

agement and promotion—cast him in the role of in-house consultant and critic."
Because of his good taste and ability to get things done, Daniels was called the
"style master of the village" by Betty Cooke.

At the same meeting, Jim Rouse reported that "The Village of Cross Keys had
478 units built or under construction with another 700 units to come." He also
made known that, subject to approval of development plans and zoning changes,
the company envisioned a 400-acre tract at the western side of the Jones Falls
Expressway near the beltway (Rockland) in Baltimore County as another residential community similar to The Village of Cross Keys. Rockland would have an
office campus, a 200-room inn and conference center, country club, 18-hole golf
course and two thousand estate-sized residential lots. The zoning was vetoed by
first term councilman, Gary Huddles.

The artificial lake at Cross Keys on whose shore the inn was to be built was
finally reduced to a sediment pond, the size of a golf green, with a fountain. Ironically this was once the water hazard for the country club golf links. A proposed
reflecting pond just west of the gatehouse never materialized. Such changes are
often made by developers because of zoning problems, economics or aesthetics.
Finally the Cross Keys Inn opened in the fall of 1965. Its 150 rooms were
trimmed to 100, but then increased before construction to 147, the number it
remains today.

Other buildings followed. The Cross Keys Tennis Club, better known as the
tennis barn, was built and opened in 1966. About the same time, the campus-
style Quadrangle, a five-building, two-story office complex, was notched into the
high schools' athletic field (the Spath Tract) on the southwest corner. "It was well
planned and landscaped and blended with its retail and residential neighbors,"
said Richard Altman.

In 1966, James W. Rouse & Company was acquired by CRD. Collectively
the companies became The Rouse Company.

The growing company had many irons in the fire. A half dozen shopping centers were simultaneously underway. Construction at Cross Keys was bustling.
And Jim was so involved with the massive Columbia project and civic activities
outside the company that investors, friends and colleagues became concerned
that the man could not maintain the pace. But Rouse still showed his optimism
in a memo written to his nephew, Bill Winstead. "My visit to Ghiradelli Square
[San Francisco] served to show me how close we now are to achieving a very
remarkable atmosphere at Cross Keys.

"We have many things going for us. First, we are blessed with one of the hap-
piest pieces of architecture we have produced anywhere. It is obvious that it has

strong and universal appeal. It is warm, intimate, friendly, fun. Also, we are off to a remarkably good start for Baltimore in having interesting shops. Octavia, The Cheese Shop, The Store Ltd., are outstanding. The Boutique is very acceptable. The Village Roost delightful. The Pharmacy, Silber's, Mollett Travel, Village Set, Carl's and the others all contribute something to the total feeling.

"In looking ahead to the expansion of the Village Square...isn't it important that we make a very big and special effort to build on what we have? We should make the same kind of try that Tommy Wolff made in producing the [sales] kiosk at Cherry Hill. We should go after small (in many cases very, very small) merchants specializing in unusual, good quality merchandise. We should search out stores in Baltimore, Washington, Philadelphia and beyond to find people who might fit. We should think of the kinds of business we would like to have and see if we can find people who are well qualified to start them here," Jim Rouse concluded.

Leasing well were the lower-priced garden apartments that provided ground floor, second and third floor units with balconies or patios. Painted board fences outlined back and side yards and special lighting at night created a warm expanse at the model homes. Large sliding doors gave all the apartments a bright and sunny look. The village's soft organic colors were used everywhere, becoming a Rouse trademark. One of Ned Daniels' favorite expressions was "Paint color is not a budget item." Toward build-out, homes were renting faster than they could be built. Hamill Court, a mid-rise apartment at the south end, opened in 1967. Finally, Jim Rouse's hope for a waiting list had materialized. "Condoizing" of Cross Keys could wait. It wouldn't be until 1981 that some of the original ninety-eight rented townhomes and some in the south end were sold as condominiums.

8

DeVito Saves the Company

Mathias J. DeVito, Rouse's dynamic heir apparent, was charmed into joining the company. "I had been a lawyer working on a number of Jim's projects while at Piper & Marbury and he asked me to come over. I was pretty successful at 38, making a lot of money back then, and I was a partner. I couldn't conceive of leaving law, but Jim kept at me, and I have to say, the things we were doing out here [with The Rouse Company] were very exciting and the things we were doing at the law firm seemed dull in comparison.

"Finally I decided to go over in the summer of 1968—got a lot of stock options that never turned out to be anything—and a lower salary. Jim was never free with money. He couldn't be. He wasn't making much money himself in those days. He did have large blocks of stock that went up, then down and then finally up again. I came in as a vice president, general counsel and secretary, then was made executive vice president in 1970." It was about the time Bill Rouse, Jim's brother, retired as chief operations officer in mid-September.

DeVito had much to keep him busy. There were three shopping centers opening in the fall of 1968, a fourth in Canada in the spring of 1969, and three others being planned in Toledo, Ohio; Echelon, New Jersey; and Austin, Texas. Columbia's development was expanding rapidly. By the end of fiscal 1968, assets of the company had passed the one billion dollar mark. And one of Jim's favorite projects, the non-profit American City Corporation, was just getting off the ground. This was a large scale urban improvement and planning organization that would counsel cities on how to renew their cores. It would eventually become a model for his Enterprise Foundation.

Matt DeVito, chairman emeritus of The Rouse Company, is said to have saved the company on three different occasions. Secretary Sharon Huffer assists him in his Cross Keys office.

Jim Rouse wanted to engage a top architect for the commercial buildings in Columbia and his condominium tower in Cross Keys. He looked around the country and counseled with leaders and building owners, contractors and even architects themselves. Mort Hoppenfeld recommended the flair of Frank O. Gehry, a Toronto, Canada, expatriate who had changed his name from Goldberg and in 1947 settled in Santa Monica, California. "When he met Rouse, the chemistry was right," said Ned Daniels of their first exposure to one another. "Rouse did voice a little concern privately that Gehry's designs might be too dramatic for the Baltimore market, but he told him to go to work." He first designed Columbia's exhibit center, then a firehouse, Merriweather Post Pavilion of Music (built as a summer home for the National Symphony) and later the company's headquarters.

Then in the late 1960s, Gehry sketched out plans for the majestic centerpiece of The Village of Cross Keys, Harper House. It would set on one of the land's highest knolls and rise fifteen floors over Jones Falls and the new expressway. This would be Jim Rouse's signature building in Cross Keys. It's budget: $12 million.

Another architect with a seemingly promising future as a staff member with The Rouse Company was interviewed and hired by Jim Rouse and Mort Hoppenfeld in their Cross Key's office on July 1, 1969. His name was "Monk," a name given by his uncle to Laurin B. Askew, Jr., at his birth. "He thought I looked like a monkey," the creative genius laughs. Monk Askew had been design director for The Rouse Company for 25 years when he left in 1999 to start his own design and planning firm. His new offices in Cross Keys are within fifty feet of where he was hired. He still does consulting work for The Rouse Company and says that Jim Rouse is responsible for renewing urban America.

Monk had been with Rouse through the rough 1970s when money was short, the economy faltering and in late 1975, when bankruptcy was a distinct possibility. He headed up a department of designers, planners and others. Their job was to conceive, layout, contract and manage "outside" architects and designers to carry forward the initial concepts of the major marketplaces The Rouse Company would create over the next three decades. "Jim was a believer that he could do anything," said Askew. "And, quite frankly, there wasn't much he couldn't do."

Money was very tight when the architectural firm of Marks & Cooke designed the lodge-like community center (now called the Village Club) to be tucked in the woods over-looking the Jones Falls. It was July 1969. Among the chaos and concern of the time, there were even rumors that The Village of Cross Keys could be for sale. A letter to Jim Rouse from commercial Realtor David W. Kornblatt, dated July 31, 1969, said he had a bank client in Washington, D.C., "who would be interested in purchasing the Cross Keys development on a cash basis. The client," the letter went on, "would be willing to pay for the potential that exists in the project, i.e., apartments and other land undeveloped." Two newspaper reporters called to say they had heard that Cross Keys was about to be sold. George M. Brady, Jr., a senior vice president and director of The Rouse Company, said in an internal memo to Jim Rouse dated August 19, "I denied that this is so and I told Dave Kornblatt that VCK [Village of Cross Keys] was not for sale." In a bold turn-around move, Brady proposed to Jim that the interested D.C. bank "may be a real source for part or all of the financing which would be needed in a month to 45 days."

It was a particularly stressful time. In December 1969, The Rouse Company began moving its staff and equipment from Cross Keys to Columbia. "Jim thought we should make a commitment to Columbia." said Ned Daniels. And as if that confusion wasn't enough, the company was choking on budgetary complexities. Some numbers weren't adding up at Cross Keys. There were questions about past operating records that didn't show a good return or were too confused. Jim Rouse got into these firestorms as they arose. He had a keen mind and years of accounting experience, and quickly made the necessary changes to stabilize the company. Once he shot off a memo to Willard, that asked "…why hadn't a written change order been issued for upgrading the wood flooring in the auditorium?" At the time the company was looking for thirty percent return on its equity.

"I was still busy making many of the plans for the Village of Cross Keys during those years," said Rich Altman. "Property had been acquired providing a total of seventy-two acres. In the beginning there was a lot of green [structures] and little gray [parking]. As time went on, there was a lot more gray and less green. Parking was not considered in the early master plan. There were buildings, roads and landscaping, but little else. Eventually residential density did change because of realities and compromise settlements with the Roland Park Civic League and the country club. Density was traded away to increase commercial development at one point in time.

"There were a number of high-rises in the Cross Keys original plan," said Altman, "three in the long-range plan. Expansion of the Village Square and the addition of Harper House eliminated two of them in favor of a higher density, low-rise plan, much of which was never executed. As an example, the two empty green hills to the north and south of the Village Square had always been earmarked for residential housing."

In the early 1970s interest rates and inflation soared, demand for new housing plummeted, and Matt DeVito was appointed president, it is said, to save the company from bankruptcy. Jim Rouse remained chair and CEO, but Matt was the one to squeeze the fat out of the struggling company and refocus its direction. He cut the staff of nine hundred in half, including Bill Finley, who had helped bring Columbia into being.

With all the back-and-forth confusion, Rich Altman kept working on a plan to construct a separate office building on what is now the parking lot between the tennis club and the inn. However, that program got caught in the downturn in the retail economy. The Village Club opened June 6, 1971, and we were going through multiple schemes for Village Square II before settling on the one that began construction after groundbreaking on October 15, 1971.

Ned Daniels, with Bill Rouse who would occasionally come out of retirement to help the company, flew to Toledo, Ohio, to sell department store officials on locating in new Rouse malls. According to Daniels, he and Bill were to meet them in a hotel lobby. Before they arrived, Bill excused himself and headed for the men's room. When the executives showed up, Ned went looking for Bill. He found him on the floor of the restroom. He had had a massive heart attack. "They took Bill to the hospital and worked on him, but he never recovered." Willard Goldsmith Rouse, Jr., died October 20, 1971. Ned immediately called Jim Rouse and told him the news. "He asked me to make arrangements through Jenkins [Baltimore funeral home] and not to have anyone do anything to the body until it arrived back in Baltimore." Then Ned arranged with Bernie Fenwick for one of his charter planes from Butler Aviation at Friendship. At six, the next evening, the aircraft landed back at the Baltimore airport and taxied up to the hanger and waiting hearse. Looking out the window of the plane Ned could see waiting on the tarmac were Bill's wife, Kitty, their four children, Jim Rouse and Dia and O'Donnell Pascault. To spare the family needless stress over seeing Bill's body under a sheet, Daniels had the pilot taxi 180 degrees around so the door would be on the opposite side where the hearse was parked.

Betty Cooke was so overwhelmed when she learned of Bill's death, she immediately planned a memorial boxwood garden for the courtyard of Village Square. It contained a dozen boxwoods that had been taken by Bill as cuttings from the gardens of Alex Brown's Mondawmin and raised at his home in Roland Park. She used those young boxwoods as the garden's centerpiece. There was a canopy of wisteria and white birch trees. Until recently, the memorial and plaque were located in front of the Cross Roads Restaurant.

On April 1, 1972, project manager Edward P. Wilmot sent a memo to Skip Cochran, Jr., at Rouse headquarters. It was marked, "Private and Confidential" and contained a status report on The Village of Cross Keys. In the two-and-a-half months Wilmot had been on the project, he said the "team had lost its Development Director, Project Architect, Project Construction Manager, Tenant Coordinator and Senior Leasing Representative. Subsequently it lost its newly assigned Construction Manager and the in-house General Contractor. We are now working with our third Construction Manager."

Whether it was the economy, the intense pressure of work, problems of construction, customer complaints, budget cuts or personnel changes, employee morale at Cross Keys was seriously low.

On June 18, 1972, more storm clouds were on the horizon. This time it was a natural disaster. Hurricane Agnes, some called "the hundred-year storm," crawled up the east coast into Chesapeake Bay. Margie Osborne and her husband, Bob, who was Baltimore's Civil Defense Director in those days, had two carloads of their kids and friends visiting their shore home on South River in Anne Arundel County. When the skies darkened and static blotted out weather reports on the radio, they started for their home in Baltimore. Light rain turned into a downpour. Dodging low spots that were already flooding, the Osbornes arrived home to their two phones ringing. The 47-year-old attorney was needed immediately at the Control Center on Coldspring Lane. With the overnight rainfall reaching over twelve inches later on Monday, plans had to be made to evacuate low-lying areas of the city.

Jones Falls was a particularly troublesome waterway. Osborne and other city officials were fearful that the ancient dam at Lake Roland would roll over or slide downstream. Twelve evacuation centers were activated. There were distant memories of major Jones Falls floods, like the one on July 24, 1868, which took out a dam along a tributary, Western Run, and water rose halfway up the storefronts that sat along Falls Road in Mt. Washington.

During Hurricane Agnes in 1972, The Village of Cross Keys was evacuated because of concerns that Lake Roland dam may slide or roll over causing disastrous flooding downstream. The Baltimore city dam was later reinforced.

As Hurricane Agnes approached Baltimore, police and firefighters were already evacuating people along the Falls including Jim Rouse's Village of Cross Keys. "It was about nine in the morning and this fireman came to our door and told us to get out," said Frank DeFilippo who lived with his wife, Beverly, in a duplex in Dunn's Grove. "I thought he was kidding and would just forget about us. We were about to go out anyway. Finally a police officer came back and threatened to arrest us if we didn't get out." There was a traffic jam in the village, everybody heading for higher ground. Fortunately for the DeFilippos and the other new residents of Cross Keys, the Lake Roland dam held. After a study by the Army Corps of Engineers declared the dam unsafe, Whitman, Requardt engineer Jack Gillett, helped design the reconstruction of the dam in the late 1980s.

"Some of original dam was built on rock with slave hands." he said. "We enlarged the spillway and resurfaced it, raised the sides to carry more water and added more concrete for weight and refurbished the valve house." With the increased silting against the bottom, things should be safe.

During the same year, a storm over matrimony caught up with Jim and Libby Rouse and they agreed to end their thirty-one year marriage. The two had been partners through much of the learning process of both marriage and building a business. Their private discussions about the business had given Jim a valuable sounding board. They had three grown children: Robin, James W., Jr., and Winstead, known as Ted, and grandchildren. Some say they noticed a difference in Jim Rouse following the turmoil of divorce and the loss of his brother. "When Bill died," said Ned Daniels, "Jim lost the brakes that were sometimes necessary to slow his compulsive actions."

After the flood of 1972, Nancy Allison, Jim Rouse's secretary, was reminded of the so-called "flood of August of 1968" when heavy rains caused several inches of water to gather in the sales office on the lower floor of the gatehouse. She had been asked to bring the problem to Jim's attention after four months of delay. Lingering dampness and foul odor from the wet carpet made the use of the office unbearable. The water was apparently leaking in from the abandoned Baltimore City Water Works conduit, possibly damaged from earlier construction work. Rouse blueprints, dated November 22, 1966, also show that the garden apartments in Fallswood I are placed on top of the "Abandon 6' 4" x 5' water tunnel," but ground and storm water still flow languidly through it.

Beginning in 1862 and continuing for the next half century, the big hand-cut rock and brick tunnel built by the "Water Works" had served all the city its potable water. One of the three valve houses and waste weirs is still standing within fifty feet of the Cross Keys gatehouse. Resembling a mausoleum and inscribed "1860," the valve house contains gears and gates that helped regulate the flow of water drawn from Lake Roland in its 3.7-mile flow along the west side of Falls Road to the semi-circular Hampden Reservoir once located at 36th Street. The reservoir (created for fire protection of Clipper and Mt. Vernon Mills in Woodberry below), was drained and is now filled by tons of expressway dirt and named Roosevelt Field. Silt and disease ended the use of water from Lake Roland in 1915.

Above: The valve house at Cross Keys was designed by James Slade and built in 1860 by John W. Maxwell & Son as part of Baltimore City's water system. Efforts are underway to restore the historic structure.
Below: Inside the valve house, gates fifteen feet below the surface could be raised and lowered to regulate the flow of water to Hampden Reservoir or Jones Falls. The conduit is over six feet in diameter.

By now Matt DeVito had settled into his job as president and was fighting problems created by the economy. While most of the components of The Village of Cross Keys had been built, the highest, largest and most expensive apartment tower was being staged in 1972. A contract was signed to allow architect Frank O. Gehry to start preliminary drawings of the new 220,000 square foot condominium tower, Harper House. It would be named after Robert Goodloe Harper on whose wheat farm The Village of Cross Keys was being built. Frank had set up a local office, Gehry, Walsh and O'Malley, in a Roland Park house now displaced by the red brick bank next to the middle school. In a full-page advertisement in the *New Yorker* magazine, Harper House was called "one of Baltimore's most distinctive and appealing residential opportunities." It boasted an unusual diverse selection of floor plans, "there are 17," it read, "including studio designs and one-, two- and three-bedroom units, plus 14 two-story penthouse residences, some with roof-top gardens, patios and solariums." And uniformed door attendants. Construction would start August 1, 1972.

Santa Monica Place was to be The Rouse Company's first shopping center in California. It had been a hard fought battle in the early 1970s. As a local businessperson, Frank Gehry was a big help, but many of the Rouse Company's top executives were required for the political maneuverings that they hoped would get it under contract. At one of the large meetings in which Jim Rouse was to make a presentation, he suddenly collapsed to the floor. Immediately he was taken to the hospital, and after a thorough examination and testing, he was told to slow down, that his condition was probably caused by exhaustion. Little concern was shown for his heavy smoking in the early days. Jerry McDermott and Scott Ditch saw that Jim was safely on the plane escorting him back to Baltimore and home.

During the 1973–75 recession, facing bankruptcy Rouse had to refinance Columbia. The story went around that Jim met with Frazar Wilde, chairman of Connecticut General Life Insurance Company and said, "I've got some good news and bad news," at which time the financier asked first for the bad news. "We can't pay on the principle or the interest," said Jim. "What's the good news?" asked Wilde to which Jim replied that he was naming a lake in Columbia after him.

The economy wasn't conducive to any expansion whatsoever so he canceled plans for two new towns, one at Shelby County Farms, next to Memphis, Tennessee, the other at Wye Island, on Maryland's Eastern Shore. Wye Island was a particularly frustrating loss for Jim Rouse, the company and its stockholders. On March 14, 1974, Jim rode into Centreville, Maryland, ready to persuade and charm a collection of tough Shoremen. After all, he was one of them, grew up just eight miles south and he was certain they would like his residential plan for Wye Island, 2,500 acres of prime real estate surrounded by forty miles of Wye River tributaries.

In the town's library, lawyers helped put together the detailed model of the new concept. Attending would be Queen Ann's County commissioners and other citizens who wanted to see what all the commotion was about. Farmers and waterman, the rich and the poor, were stiffened for the Rouse team proposal ever since his option to buy the island for $8.85 million first appeared in the local newspaper. Doug Godine and Scott Ditch, both officers in the company, had made regular visits to the Shore to try to soften up the locals. They told them of all the time and money Rouse was willing to pour into the project just to make certain the Wye Island development would be acceptable and compatible with man, beast and the environment. Jim Rouse really wanted this project. It would be a thorough endeavor and he was willing to invest $111 million in it.

Forty-five minutes later, the meeting was over. No local was budging for the hottest team in the development business. The natives didn't want more "chickenneckers" crabbing off their bridges, tossing beer cans and trash. They had turned their collective noses up at national parkland designation and certainly no "row houses" like Jim Rouse "put up in Columbia" would ever see the light of day on Wye Island. Time was running out for the normally ebullient Rouse. After ten months of hard work, he called it quits. The deal was as dead as the oyster bars off the proposed Wye Village. At a meeting of Rouse Company shareholders in the following fall, someone stood up and asked Jim how much the aborted Wye Island development had cost the company. "Between $800,000 and $900,000," he answered. Altogether the options and expenses at Shelby Farms and Wye Island amounted to $4.2 million.

Less than two months after Rouse backed-off, there were seven lucky persons who bought parcels sold at auction July 20, 1974. Several years later, at the urging of wealthy landowners in the region around the island, the state of Maryland bought Wye Island for $5.3 million.

As a leader in its field, The Rouse Company always had trouble with copycats. "I guess that's the price you pay if you're the leader in any field," said Monk Askew. "Jim used to get angry at people who came to the company, learned how to do it, then would leave and go into competition. Mike Spear and I would go somewhere to make a new business presentation and, nine times out of ten, as we were leaving, there would be former Rouse employees as consultants going in right behind us. Some, we were told, actually used photographs of our projects as their own. It really confused the decision makers."

Monk Askew worked on Phase II of Cross Key's Village Square and he also created the site plan for Harborplace in Baltimore while working closely with the late Cambridge (Massachusetts) architect Benjamin Thompson who had done the building design work for Rouse on Faneuil Hall and Harborplace. "He was very creative, an excellent designer," said Monk, "and did a lot of his concept work using photographs to project and image. We use a similar technique today with photos and the computer. And whatever we do, is often a direct descendent of The Village of Cross Keys. "As an example, that panel over there," he said motioning to a wall of colorful site plans, "is for a project in Scottsdale, Arizona. Like Cross Keys, it's open air, one-level retail, department stores, offices, a hotel, restaurants and residential, but on a larger 160-acre location. As if underlining the work of his staff, Monk said, "The Rouse Company has always been a "hands-on" client, particularly in the area of design. The outside architects give the projects, not only their legal imprimatur, but they bring fresh ideas to the table as well."

There was a huge confusion over a new project in Norfolk. Monk Askew did the basic concept even though there were questions about its viability. In 1974 Jim Rouse had met Patricia Traugott, a socialite and former housing commissioner of Norfolk. The company was getting pressure from Jim to do it even though market research said it didn't make economic sense. There weren't enough potential at that point and The Rouse Company was just beginning to figure out what the "Harbor Places" of the world needed in the way of customers to make them successful. The company finally pulled out of Norfolk.

Following their marriage, Jim and Patty Rouse moved into a five-bedroom home overlooking Wilde Lake in Columbia. They kept a telescope in the living room for watching waterfowl. Although there was no corporate jet or chauffeur-driven limousine, Jim and Patty had little time to enjoy the simpler things in life. Too many meetings, too many phone conferences. He did enjoy cooking, especially his favorite dish, Maryland terrapin, and mock turtle, made with muskrats until trapping them was outlawed. Together they sometimes managed to play tennis, jog, canoe, fish and "mess about" on their thirty-seven foot, wooden workboat named *Adequate*. It got its name from his brother-in-law O'Donnell Pascault who scolded Jim for taking friends in a small runabout across open Miles River to get to his hunting cabin at Long Point. "Why don't you get something adequate," he said.

At this point in his life, Jim Rouse was a man worth twenty-five million, but he couldn't buy any spare time, "soft time," as he called it, for his family. It is said to be one of the things that broke up his first marriage. Some say he had a far ranging intellect, but that he never read a complete book without it having a bottom line. It's easy to understand why. Consider Jim Rouse's schedule outlined by writer Mark Cohen in a story for *Baltimore Magazine*. "It's an evening when he is tied up in a meeting upstairs [in his 6th floor office] until 7, has to meet some people at the house at 7:05, fly to Richmond three hours later for meetings in the morning; then on to New York in the early afternoon, and back to Dulles for a 7 flight to London the next night."

Because Harper House would be several years in construction, it was decided to put up several model apartments to give prospective customers an idea of what they'd be buying. Whether it was the mobile home-like building that enclosed the sample apartments or their location at the corner of Hamlet Hill Road and the construction entrance, sales didn't go well. The whole idea had been to get commitments on a good share of the apartments before financing was arranged. Without the endorsements Harper House still moved ahead.

As The Village of Cross Keys development neared completion and Columbia was out of the ground, The Rouse Company was spreading its wings around the east coast, but in the south those wings were getting clipped. "In Fort Lauderdale, we learned a big lesson," said Matt DeVito. "We had a wonderful plan for an urban center and, in effect, tried to force it on the city. The lesson: You can't do anything in center city without the mayor—a strong mayor leading the charge. Fort Lauderdale became a political quagmire and we got out of it.

"Boston's Faneuil Hall Marketplace was a different story," said DeVito. "It was 1973 and Mayor Kevin White and architect Ben Thompson wanted us to do the job. Jim was ecstatic when he saw the old derelict buildings, just filled with history and potential for development." And Ben was known for being able to bring out the potential of an old building or piece of land.

The Boston deal was so loaded with politics there were times when tremendous pressures were placed on Jim Rouse. Twice he nearly lost the project. During one of the on-and-off again negotiations, Mayor White turned to Jim and said, "I hear you're like a bulldozer. If you want to get something, you push over everything to get it." Jim quickly replied, "That's not fair. If I am trying to do something and I think it is right, then I do my best to persuade other people that it right." Dia used to tell him, "To get your way in life, you have to fight." Maryland Governor Marvin Mandel once turned down one of Jim's requests simply "because he expects to get everything he wants."

DeVito continued: "In Boston, we did have a battle with the preservationists who wanted to turn the place into a museum. The first part we opened was the Quincy Market building, a tiny project. We hadn't even started the other two adjacent buildings, but when the market opened on August 26,1976, it was swarmed with people. Obviously there was a place for what Rouse wanted to do in the center city."

"It was the success of Faneuil Hall that led us to The Gallery at Market East in Philadelphia," said DeVito. "It also was another center city shopping center." As Baltimore's inner harbor was cleared of old buildings, the bare land began to show a new potential. Mayor William Donald Schaefer was getting excited. Rouse was originally offered the option to convert the long-abandoned Baltimore Gas & Electric power plant, but he refused. Jim wanted to use the 3.2 acres of public land at the strategic corner of the Inner Harbor. He asked Bob Embry, Jay Brodie, then Schaefer, if he could make a proposal. He had shown his skills in malls built around the country. "No one had been willing to risk time, money and reputation on Baltimore," he said. "People were still laughing to think the city could ever prosper as a tourist destination."

"Mayor Schaefer himself needed some convincing that what we do would work in his city," said DeVito. "Schaefer has terrific instincts. He knew he had the most valuable three acres on the waters edge. He knew if the site was going to be trusted to a developer, it would have to be done right.

"We took Schaefer and his entourage to Faneuil Hall and he took lots of photographs. Then he decided he wanted the project, so we built him a $30,000 model." Schaefer had predicted the Rouse plan would meet with ferocious opposition. People were getting to like the open vistas of the inner harbor. It became a new feature in itself. Then Councilman George Della set up an organization to stop the Rouse plan. All the time, Della was planning his own inner harbor project, a mid-rise condo building that would have spoiled the view of many of his constituents on East Montgomery Street, whose homes over-looked the harbor and skyline. That project was defeated, but in November 1979, a referendum on the Rouse plan won the voter's approval. And they elected Schaefer for a third term.

Mayor William Donald Schaefer and Jim Rouse were responsible for building the jewel on the Chesapeake known as Harborplace. It outdrew Disney World tourists by the end of its first year.——James K. Lightner

"There were some people who would not support the concept for a long time," said DeVito. "After the two marketplace pavilions were opened July 2, 1980, we had to fight other developers for the 400,000 sq. ft. Gallery, at Pratt and Light. By then Schaefer was governor and it had become somewhat fashionable in the development community to do downtown work. We got the Gallery at Harborplace, and with it the 570-room Renaissance Hotel and office tower," he said.

"I was still young when Jim indicated that he would be retiring from the presidency and CEO at sixty-five, and that was good news to me since I was anxious to run the company myself. He was like Cal Ripkin and I was the new third baseman. I was ambitious and I was ready.

"We had it all worked out—had been working on the transition for about four years. By this time, Jim didn't want to stay and thwart my career. He knew I had earned the right to run the company. The move would also give him the opportunity to do other things which he now wanted to do."

Matt DeVito's first annual meeting was with some five hundred shareholders on May 29, 1979. It was a special occasion, marking the company's beginning in Baltimore forty years earlier. The meeting was also Jim Rouse's last day as chief executive officer, although he would continue as chairman of the board until the mandatory retirement age of seventy which he'd reach in six years.

DeVito reported the 1978 financial results: net earnings were $5.9 million. Every operating division had broken its own record. Conservatively estimated current value of assets was $662 million. Shareholders' equity on a cost basis was $27 million. On a current-value basis it was $196 million. The company's work force had grown to 3,000.

At the same stockholders meeting James W. Rouse turned over the presidency to Matt DeVito with three symbols of office. The first was a Bible inscribed from Jim.

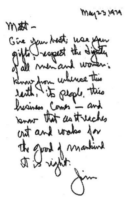

Jim Rouse wrote his thoughts in a Bible he presented to Matt DeVito when he became president and CEO of The Rouse Company.—Matt DeVito

"He didn't sit there for weeks composing that inscription," said DeVito. "It's a good demonstration of his feeling and his ability to use the English language." The second symbol of office was a framed message that read: 'When life gives you lemons, make lemonade." The third was a card that had long stood on Rouse's desk that bore Chicago architect Daniel H. Burnham's words which, in part, read, "Make no little plans. They have no magic to stir men's blood. Make big plans; aim high in hope and work...."

Then Jim Rouse would leave day-to-day work at The Rouse Company and begin plans for his Enterprise Foundation. The mission of the Enterprise Foundation was "to see that all low-income people in the United States have the opportunity for fit and affordable housing and to move up and out of poverty into the mainstream of American life." Within the next two decades, Enterprise grew to more than 2,200 members representing 800 cities across the United

States and Puerto Rico. In April 1982, however, the Enterprise Development Corporation was unveiled which would be both a blessing and a curse. While the non-profit foundation dolled out money and organized housing for the poor, the for-profit development corporation was to be its money tree.

In its first year of operation, The Rouse Company's Harborplace attracted over eighteen million people. Many were tourists, underscoring Mayor Schaefer's pledge that "someday tourists will spend their vacations in Baltimore." In that same inaugural year, it earned $42 million, created 2,300 jobs, and paid the city $1.1 million in taxes. Baltimore's harborside playground had more visitors than Disney World. For his urban renewal concepts, Master Planner James Rouse was put on the cover of *Time* magazine, August 24, 1981. It's bold headline: CITIES ARE FUN! Inside the story was packed with glowing reports about the "visionary urban builder." There was even a sidebar about his new best friend, William Donald Schaefer.

These were good times, too, for The Village of Cross Keys. The new community was called "one of the most profitable centers in Maryland on the basis of sales per square foot," in a report issued by Warren Wilson, assistant research director for The Rouse Company.

Perhaps no one knew Jim Rouse, the businessman, better than Matt DeVito. "We spent nearly two decades together," said the chairman emeritus recently. "Jim Rouse was unique. I have seen him speaking on videotapes kept in the archives, and somehow the real Jim does not get beyond the camera lens. In real life, Jim spoke with conviction and his charisma and passion and—whether it was a large group or a small gathering—Jim could reach whoever it was to heighten their response. He was incomparable.

"People say he was a visionary, but that wasn't exactly Jim either. In my view, his genius was his ability to gather ideas from whatever source—he was always on the prowl for new ideas—develop a plan and articulate them convincingly to others. His great gift was to recognize good thoughts and understand emerging concepts and be able to put them together in a rational way. And he could bring people on board with him, whether it was to put their money into the company or a project or put their lives into it. He could draw people to his ideas through his extraordinary sense of persuasion. He was just simply magical in that way.

"He hated the term, salesman, and it wasn't the appropriate word, but Jim *was* a great salesman. He doesn't deserve the term, for it belittles him in many ways. But if you wanted to simplify it all, you could say Jim's ability to persuade was extraordinary."

DeVito continued: "Jim Rouse was the center of attention whenever he was in a room with people. Silence was not part of the guy. That's not to say he was loquacious; he was a good listener, but he was always willing to contribute.

"There was a difficult time for all of us when everything started falling apart for the company in the seventies. I thought it was a remarkable era, but it took time for Jim to overcome one negative situation after another. The people he had persuaded to buy the stock or put money into Columbia somehow turned on him when the economy faltered, as though *he* was responsible for it. He was hung out to dry. There's nothing worse than a fallen angel.

"We had been selling The Rouse Company on the highest principles of morality and financial strength and promise," said DeVito. "But we had expanded into endeavors that were beyond our basic business and in which we had little experience. That really got us into trouble. Jim was a superb businessman and very astute financially, but a real risk taker and at times he could be unfocused. He could be strong—tough as nails—but compassionate. He would say, 'That was a bad idea; we wasted a lot of money. Then follow-up with, 'Let's forget about it,' just like that—if he had the confidence in the person.

"In those trying times, sad to say, many people who were earlier mesmerized by his wonderful ability, turned on him. He never knew that as much as I did because, maybe out of raw respect, they never expressed their unhappiness directly to him. But those of us trying to restore confidence in the company, saw it. The down side didn't last long, because after the economy improved, Jim was ready with new ideas. We were a great team. Together we pulled the company out of trouble.

Under Jim's rein, The Rouse Company revenues had grown at an annualized rate of fourteen percent. He stayed on the company board as chairman for five more years. "Jim came to the board meetings, was wonderfully supportive, but by then he and Patty Rouse were deeply into Enterprise Foundation, and its subsidiary the Enterprise Development Corporation which was creating small retail projects in the image of Harborplace. The development company created the profit fuel that powered the non-profit foundation. Gradually it became apparent that there was growing friction between Enterprise Development and The Rouse Company," said DeVito. "In the view of the board, Jim was building projects in competition with the company. Jim defended himself by saying they were small, but, indeed, some could have been of interest to the company. And because he was still chairman of the board of The Rouse Company, a great deal of confusion was being created. Many people believed that Enterprise Development was a Rouse Company subsidiary and that its projects were ours.

"In 1984, at age seventy, Jim was required to retire from the board of directors of The Rouse Company. I wouldn't characterize his leaving as acrimonious, but it wasn't a happy time. I continued to serve on the board of Enterprise and as much as I cared for and understood Jim, and he cared for me, still there was some lingering tension. After that, Enterprise had its problems and at one point I asked Jim if we could take it over and run it out, but he refused."

9

The Flawed House

The design work architect Frank O. Gehry did for the Harper House high-rise had been very good for its era. It was safe, meaning nothing dramatic. His work in Columbia and Cross Keys was good enough for The Rouse Company to hire him for Santa Monica Place in California. "Matt DeVito was a real believer in Frank," said Monk Askew. On his visit to the coast for the opening of Santa Monica Place in 1981, the young Gehry didn't seem happy. It was a melancholy that Matt had noticed before. Finally he asked Frank, who considered Matt his mentor, if he had a problem. "I guess I just don't like working on your project [Santa Monica Place]," he said. "I have no freedom to do anything I really want to do. And the money…."

"Well I think you should quit doing commercial buildings and do what you want to do," advised DeVito. Gehry later, in a *New Yorker* magazine article, attributed Matt's fatherly advice for getting him on the road to success. But one major obstacle stood in his way.

In mid-1980, water leaks were becoming intolerable for some residents of Harper House. Al Kilberg, a resident in the condo for years who lived through the leaks and re-facing of the building, still gets chills when he thinks what residents went through. "I understand the "curtain-wall" [brick veneer] and mortar system was copied from a building in California and Rouse hired the architect," he said. "We found there were code problems when the folks on the top floors were getting soaked walls, rugs and carpets every time it rained."

Finally, one of the residents, H. Donald Glaser, a retired engineer with time on his hands, looked into the construction and took photographs which showed that apparently some of the brick ties (corrugated steel straps) meant to join the building's steel studs to the wet mortar between the bricks were improperly attached. In addition to cavities in the mortar, the building's steel frame wasn't rigid enough. Any flex caused cracks along the mortar joints. *Warfield's* newspaper reported that Max Israelson, an original condo unit owner, was one of the first plaintiffs in a series of lawsuits that began in the late 1980s.

"At a symposium with the architect, Harper House residents were asked to submit questions dealing with any aspect of the building or renovation," said Kilberg. "We brought in our own inspectors to watch every step of reconstruction. We were told they brought down the same scaffolding that was used to clean the Statue of Liberty for the Bicentennial. We had to live with boarded-up windows, noise and shuttle parking. It was a nightmare for over three years. But today we probably have the best constructed building in Baltimore City," said Kilberg.

Clad in scaffolding once used to restore the Statue of Liberty, brick facing of Harper House was replaced among other changes required by residents' lawsuit. The repairs took nearly three-and-a-half years to complete.—Craig Daniels

Periodically, during the re-building process, The Rouse Company sent updates to residents to keep them informed. One published on October 20, 1988 read: "As you know, we entered into an agreement with the Council of Unit

Owners for Harper House Condominium ("Association") to perform certain repairs to the Harper House building. The repairs include the erection of scaffolding around Harper House and the removal and replacement of the brick exterior with a strengthened brick wall. The brick removal has been completed on the north and west sides (Phase I) of the building. New brick has been replaced on the 3rd through 12th floors and is in progress on the 2nd and 13th floors. The windows are currently being installed on the 7th through 12th floors. Garage repairs are also in progress. Phase I scaffolding removal is scheduled to start in December. A shuttle service to parked vehicles is being provided for Harper House residents whose vehicles cannot be located in the garage or temporary parking facilities while the garage is being repaired."

According to *Engineering News Record*, Rouse's construction subsidiary, The Village of Cross Keys, Inc., had to sue the architects, Frank O. Gehry & Associates, as well as the general contractor, R. M. Shoemaker Co., and U. S. Gypsum. An out-of-court settlement was reached with the apartment owners. DeVito said the company got some money from the Gehry organization, but that the building contractor was only a shell. He thought Rouse got hit for about $15 million. Others have said the cost to tear off the old brick, replace the windows, sliding glass doors, repair the balconies and re-brick the skin of the building correctly, plus re-pour concrete for the underground garage and outdoor plazas was closer to twice that much. "It was ugly...very ugly," said one Rouse insider.

The Harper House reconstruction process began in April 1987. It took nearly three-and-a-half-years to complete. Thirty years after he worked on Harper House, Frank O. Gehry designed one of the most notable buildings in the world, the Guggenheim Museum in Bilbao, Spain. Today he is considered the foremost living architect in the world.

"My relationship with Jim Rouse and the experiences—good and bad—were some of the most precious and important ones in my life," said Matt DeVito. "He broadened my scope and changed the way I looked at things. He was a wonderful example for leading a good and productive life, and I miss him very much."

One of the great tragedies in The Rouse Company was when its president and CEO, Mike Spear, was killed in 1990 trying to land his twin-engine Piper Cheyenne II near Logan Airport in Boston. He went off the radar screen and crashed between two houses. Spear, with an architectural education, had come up through the company first as a summer intern while in college, later as head of marketing research, then became general manager at Cross Keys, then Columbia, after which he went back inside the corporation as a senior officer. When DeVito retired, he took over the leadership of the company. Besides Spear, the crash also killed his wife and second oldest daughter. "It was very very sad," said Monk Askew. "He was a good friend. Matt DeVito was called back for another year and helped keep the company on track. He also brought decorum to the company." It's been said that over his tenure, DeVito saved the company on three different occasions.

The Rouse Company has grown. It is big. There are elegant shopping malls all over the country and offices to service them. Headquarters are still in Columbia, Maryland, but the new town is changing, too. The shopping centers are being sold off. The last village, River Hill, began construction in 1998. And long ago, back in the early 1970s, the company realized that hotels and inns were better and more profitable if run by the large chains. While future projects may include residential housing, the construction will be done by a select group of home-builders. This would eliminate complaints from homeowners, some justified, many not. Even the notable residents of Cross Keys had their words. Take Ogden Nash who in 1970 put his concerns in verse:

Unfair! Unfair!

I wish to scotch the rumor that

I am the enemy of the cat.

I guess that no one on this globe

is less of an aleurophobe,

In spite of which I hate the feline

That for my warblers makes a beeline,

Whose owner turns it loose to prey

On nuthatch, cardinal, junco, jay,

Whose ancient hunting urge is stirred

By sight of dove or mocking bird,

Who spurns its Puss-in-Boots to speed

To where I've scattered sunflower seed.

Three cats there are which haunt the scene

At Number 30 Olmsted Green;

One gray, one black, one black and white,

All insolence and appetite.

Like witches at Walpurgis party,

To them "Scat!" simply means "Eat hearty!"

Here cats walk wild, but dogs on leashes.

Are cats a special privileged species?

A Plaintive Plaintiff

My viewing has a restricted view:

Channels 13, 11, 2.

I hope that some day ere my burial

I'll be allowed a rooftop aerial.

Ogden Nash did have legitimate complaints about his new townhouse at 30 Olmsted Green. In a letter to Jim Rouse, dated January 24, 1969, he wrote: "Dear Mr. Rouse, As we near the end of our 4th year at Cross Keys there are several pieces of business that I must bring up. First, but not for the first time, the TV situation. It is highly irritating to spend more than $500 on a set and find the reception limited to the 3 local channels whose programming is deplorable while friends in other parts of Baltimore and in the valley are getting the good network programs from Washington and even Lancaster simply because of outside aerials." Nash's other complaints involved parking spaces, sliding doors and a faulty rain spout. In yet another letter he said the dishwasher was breaking his wife's valuable china. His hand-written correspondence on his personal letterhead was always signed "Very Sincerely, Ogden Nash."

Probably no more than twenty percent of the original shops are still in the Village Square. Many couldn't suffer the high rents, others passed on to larger quarters and still others were just under-capitalized. Most of those who left the Square were quickly replaced. There was always attention to the merchant mix, always until recently, when more desperate motivation has caused flirtation with more chain stores, seldom before considered by Rouse management. In the Fall of 2002, two new women's clothing stores and an art gallery were added, nearly filling the available space in the center.

Perhaps the most devastating loss to the village was the closing in 1994 of The Village Food Center, better known as the Cross Keys Deli. Opened twenty years earlier, the center served mouth-watering cold beef, hand-cut Western fries, pans of macaroni and cheese that made the eatery a Baltimore institution. Irv Folk and Morris Tossman started the deli. It was virtually Cross Key's publicity generator. All sorts of celebrities were seen having a quick sandwich or an ice tea, relaxed, conversing with friends. Oprah Winfrey, a resident who at the time was a television reporter for WJZ, loved the fried chicken. Howard Cosell, Katherine Hepburn, Ella Fitzgerald, Reggie Jackson and Supreme Court Justice Thurgood Marshall and a host of other celebrities found charm and quality in the place. Local media personalities from TV Hill were always catching lunch there. The visiting football and baseball teams liked the remoteness of the inn; still kids swarmed the deli for their autographs. When the new stadiums arrived, the teams sought lodging downtown. While retirement of the principals was the reason given for closing after twenty years, the Cross Keys Deli opened in Timonium within the year.

The south parcel, called the "South Hill," was given to the Cross Keys community in exchange for approval of Roland Green, the new controversial cluster of sixteen townhomes that were built on the "North Hill," four acres of what many considered the front lawn of Harper House. Offered at a cost ranging from $350,000 to $750,000, the homes were first announced by the builder as being constructed of brick, cedar and glass. When Ed Gunts of the *Sun* wrote about it after its 1999 opening, he said the exteriors were "clad in brick and glass," as though the more expensive and attractive "cedar" may have been left out at the last minute. In fact, the majority of the exteriors is not cedar, but synthetic siding. Still, the homes are much enjoyed by their owners. Some people attribute their lack of architectural compatibility to the existing townhomes to a "lapse in judgment by Rouse internal management who had lost the vision and put more emphasis on land sales and cash."

Over the years, there have been changes in the management of Cross Keys. The Village Management today is a freestanding corporation that keeps all the working parts operating. It provides administrative staff at its offices in the Village Club. Under a special arrangement, it also manages other apartments and condominiums in the Baltimore area. The total organization of The Village of Cross Keys can be found in the Appendix.

It was spring of 1992, at a cocktail party for the board of directors meeting in Columbia, that the normally ebullient and fidgety Jim Rouse, 78, felt a low-level pain in his chest, followed by perspiration and a feeling of faintness. Immediately Bob Keidel and Dave Tripp drove him to the emergency room at nearby Howard County General where he met his friend, Dr. Mike Kelenem. The physician noted an arterial blockage and sent Rouse on to Johns Hopkins Hospital in Baltimore. Further tests were made revealing blockage of five arteries.

On Saturday, May 23, Dr. Bruck Reitz, director of cardiac surgery at Hopkins, spent four hours inside Jim's chest cavity replacing arteries with veins in a quintuple bypass. Jim remembers there was "no significant suffering from the massive wrench of my body," he wrote to a friend. "Minor aches and pain from cutting and stretching, but the only residual has been exhaustion, inertia, no energy, physical or mental, with the assurance that all will be well." Rouse recovered slowly from his bypass surgery and was working from his home by July.

The old workhorse had lost a lot of weight during his recovery. There was time to think about his first child, Robin, who was seriously ill. And the stress of Enterprise was getting more difficult to handle, although his wife Patty was at his side to offer protection from over-work. Then in a more or less routine visit to his doctor, Jim was diagnosed with Lou Gehrig's disease. It was a devastating blow to the man who could, and did, handle every burden life threw at him. It was just another problem to solve. This time, however, his debilitation was overwhelming and time was painfully running out.

On April 9, 1996, came the phone calls, e-mails and faxes. Wire services flashed the story. Jim Rouse had died. He was 81. The next day there was an enormous outpouring of tributes and happy remembrances from a world of those who mourned his passing.

Over 3,600 persons: family, friends, politicians from the ranks of the nation, states and cities attended the two services, one at Brown Memorial Presbyterian in Baltimore and later that afternoon at Merriweather Post Pavilion in Columbia. Television and radio carried special acknowledgements. Full pages of stories about the life of this urban design genius filled the print media. *The New York Times* called James Wilson Rouse "a man who sought not just to make profits but to transform the landscape and the quality of civic life."

"Spiritually," said C. William Struever, a Baltimore developer deeply influenced by Jim Rouse, "he was one of the most important people in America—giving us the courage and boldness to take on our toughest problems. He knew no despair. He was constantly getting fired up…to take on the impossible and make it happen."

In the next week's issue of *Newsweek*, Malcolm Jones, Jr., wrote "With the cold eye of an accountant, the touch of Midas and the heart of a Sunday-school teacher, Rouse radically altered America's assumptions about suburbs and cities. Preaching the gospel of doing well by doing good, he became one of the most influential (and most imitated) social engineers of his time."

The Village of Cross Keys, the most successful residential and commercial community in Baltimore City, showing the Harper House high-rise and many of the other living styles which are home to some 5,000 persons in over 1,200 dwelling units.—James K. Lightner

10

The Villages and Their Futures

The two villages of Cross Keys have lived totally different lives, yet there is a thread of continuity between them. Perhaps it is their mutual relationship to Roland Park and Robert Goodloe Harper that have transferred their strength and culture to both of them. It can be argued that the original village was imprisoned by Roland Park's need for domestic help and that as long as that need was dominant, the African Americans would remain static in their plight.

None of those who have used African American "help" can deny there is a sense of the "old plantation," when the young black women serve our buffets and the black men, our cocktails. It grants us a feeling of success. And that feeling was only possible when we were able to show dominance and importance by hiring those whom we thought to be inferior, but worthy of our attention. It is a southern thing. And in those earliest days, Roland Park was southern and, for the most part, Confederate in its beliefs.

Among those who recognized the need to help their "servants" beyond a weekly stipend were a Roland Park judge, a television personality, and an arts matron—all living in Roland Park—who went beyond money to guide and uplift those who lived below on the "Road" in Cross Keys Village.

At times, the original black community was criticized by the white establishment that surrounded it. Often boisterous, sometimes independent, and later, actually too late to save the village, African American leadership began to emerge, change and flourish as the new professionals within the Greater Baltimore community.

With all but eleven of its seventy-six homes destroyed in the name of progress, one more burned in May of 2002 and four more of those remaining will soon be leveled and replaced with a modern office building. Ironically, it may be developed by African Americans. And rightly so, at the hands of a direct descendant of Tobias Scott whose memory was such an integral part of the original village. One home at 4713 Falls Road, by some considered to be the oldest still standing, will continue as a residence and, with good fortune, could become an historical representative of what used to be, what used to provide the love and respect of family.

We should point out, too, that both Cross Keys Village and The Village of Cross Keys have been racially integrated, at least by a few of both races, from the beginning. Each place has proved that people *can* live and progress together. Geraldine Epps who was raised in Cross Keys Village gave a salute to the philosophy of Jim Rouse. "I used to work at the Cross Keys Inn at a time Mr. Rouse owned it," she said. "When he learned that someone needed a down payment or financing to buy a home, he arranged for it. He also presented college scholarship grants for my two daughters. Both of them are now successful women in Baltimore business." Jim Rouse was true to his heart. He believed he could make a difference, to help people "struggling to survive in miserably unfit housing, in wretched, disorderly neighborhoods with too little food, too little health care...too little happiness, too little hope."

The "new" Village of Cross Keys, like Roland Park, has done well in its years of existence. Roland Park still attracts quality families, and homes are constantly undergoing renovations and real estate values continue to escalate. The same is true of The Village of Cross Keys, the dream of an urban paradise that Jim Rouse saw as the model for his new town of Columbia.

Residents agree that The Village of Cross Keys endures and truly is a paradise. It's close to downtown Baltimore City and has all the amenities. It's quiet and secure. And while the retail shop owners have their ups and downs, most like the environment and plan to stay in the Village Square. Jim Rouse used to say "Retailing is a democracy. The consumers vote with their purchases." The Rouse Company still owns forty-six percent of The Village of Cross Keys and has plans to someday expand the office and parking space in a mid-rise building to be constructed on the open lot between the tennis barn and the Radisson Hotel. There are other changes that will enhance and carry The Village of Cross Keys forward through the twenty-first century. And the memories of the original 200-year-old Cross Keys Village will always enhance our future. Maybe Jim Rouse actually did know he was naming his urban community after, not just an ancient inn, but a vibrant community of African Americans.

APPENDIX

Each house is numbered from 1 to 74 starting a bottom right. See resident names on next page.

155

Occupants of Dwellings and Commercial Properties in African American Cross Keys Village

Falls Road, East Side
1 Baker *(White)*
   Williams

White Oak Grove
2 Hawkins
3 Lipscomb

Falls Road, East Side
4 Bettie's Beer Garden
   (Second Floor)
   Scott, Arthur & Bettie
   Edward Smiths
5 Webster*
   Champ
6 Samuel Brown*
   Douglas
7 Hughes*
   Marshall Stewart
8 Grocery Store*
   Parker Douglas
9 Falls Road AME Church
10 Jones
   Scott Behind Church
11 Brown
   Hall
12 Chase
13 Johnnie Brown

Spath Lane
14 Wilson
   Epps
15 (Unknown)
16 Garrett
17 Stokes

Falls Road, East side
18 Diggs
19 Smith, Etta & Sylvester
20 Lee, Monroe & Violet
21 McGraw
   Simon Scotts
22 Fuller
   Young
23 Clair
   Rice
24 Harriday
25 Lee
   Epps
26 Johnson
   Handy-Herbert
27 Johnson
   Harvey

Oakdale Road
28 Lynch, Charles & Edith
   Smith, Robert & Lula
   Lee, Emanuel & Lurinda

29 Taylor, Mary Ellen
   Johnson, Edgar & Ann
30 Spivey
   Pettus
   Walton
31 Sparrow
   Handy

Falls Road, East Side
32 Tyson AUMP Church
33 Parker*
   Scott
34 Lee, Norbert & Eleanor*
   Brown
   McBride
35 Clay*
36 Kutch*
   Crosby
37 Lee, George & Lillian
   Coulter
38 Scott*
   Francis
39 Preston*

Falls Road, West Side
40 Benjamin Brown
41 Lee, William & Vivian
   Graham
   Mebane, James & Rosa

42 Moore, Edward & Alexander
43 Bond
44 Frederick *(White)*
   Wyatt
45 Lee, George & Lillian
   Tate
   Joyner
46 Hynson
   Hammond
47 Lovett *(White)*
   Hall-Turner
48 Underwood *(White)*
   Garrett
49 Boyer
   Ringgold
50 Turner
   West
51 Brown, Charles & Lydia
   Bryant
52 Anderson
   Holt
   Bert Simmons
53 Jones, Annie & Franklin
   Gaskins
54 Sidney Henry-Webster
   Holt
55 Jones, Charles & Maude
56 White
   Roland Scott

57 West
   Hall
58 Elementary School No. 158
59 Lee, Emanuel & Lurinda
   Frey
60 McBride
61 Jones
62 Walton
   Lee
   Turner
   Merritt
63 Brown, George & Mary
64 Parker
   Franklin
65 Matthews
66 Hurt, Edward & Ada
67 Handy
   Herbert

68 Faulkner
   Walton
69 Hawkins
70 Green
   Thomas
71 Stewart
   Kennedy
72 Lessinger *(White)*
   Howard Hawkins
73 Stokes
74 Frederick *(White)*
   Pulley

*Still Standing

List compiled by Paul M. Johnson, July 2002.

BUILDINGS AND MANAGEMENT OF THE VILLAGE OF CROSS KEYS

Operation and management of the 689 townhomes, garden homes, mid-rises and Harper House are governed by the following nine separate self-governing associations:

- 98 units in Condominium I (includes Palmer Green, Bouton Green Olmsted Green and the townhomes along Hamlet Hill Road, all in the north end)

- 17 units, Roland Mews (north end townhomes)

- 16 units, Roland Green (north end townhomes)

- 126 units, Dunn's Grove (north end garden apartments)

- 81 units, Fallswood I (south end garden apartments)

- 66 units, Fallswood II (south end garden apartments)

- 50 units, Goodlow House (north end mid-rise)

- 40 units, Hamill Court (south end mid-rise)

- 195 units, Harper House (north end high-rise)

Each of these nine condominium associations is governed by elected boards of directors.

Organizational Abbreviations of The Village of Cross Keys

VCKI—Village of Cross Keys, Inc., subsidiary of The Rouse Company that owns and operates the commercial areas and certain common tracts and security.

CKMC—Cross Keys Maintenance Corporation is comprised of nine condominium associations, plus The Rouse Company and the Radisson Hotel. It owns and maintains most common areas such as lawns, trees, main roads, most sidewalks, paths, lighting, swimming pools, outdoor tennis courts,

Club House, gatehouse and valve house. A portion of homeowners' fees goes toward covering these costs.

VMI—Village Management, Inc., an independent management company that leases space in the Village Club House to provide management and maintenance services to CKMC and certain other condo associations outside Cross Keys.

VMI Contracting Division—Registered contractors provide home improvements and repairs to residents of Cross Keys.

Village Square shops and offices, Quadrangle offices, Gatehouse and Tennis Club are owned and operated by The Village of Cross Key, Inc. The Radisson Hotel is managed by Interstate Hotels & Resorts.

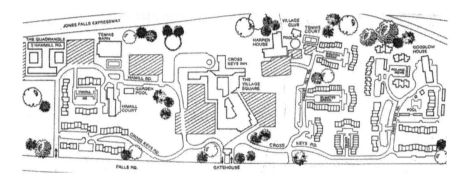

The Cross Keys Village built by The Rouse Company, 1961–1975.

CROSS KEYS SHOPS, PAST AND PRESENT

Ann Taylor
Benetton
Benson Optical
Bibelot
Bon Voyage
Book Bag
Bowers & Snyder
Brentano's Roten Collection
Bun Penny
Café Dubray
Caprice
Captain's Wines and Liquors
Carl Intercoiffure
Cheese Shop
Chequers, Ltd.
Chezelle
Chico's
Child's Play
Circa
Columbia Bank
Corner Sweet
Crazy Carrot
Crepe du Jour
Cross Keys Barbaria
Cross Keys Cleaners, Coblers, Tailors
Cross Keys Health & Wellness Center
Cross Keys Inn

Cross Keys Pharmacy
Crosspatch
Crossroads Restaurant
Donna's
Downs Engravers and Stationers
Equitable Bank, N. A.
Fancy Work
Fancy Works
Flower Cart
Flowers & Fancies
French Bread Factory
Gazelle, Ltd.
George Howard
Georgetown Lear Design
Grand Style Gallery
Growing Up Shop
H.C. Garthe Co.
Heirloom Jewels
Hess for Her
Irresistibles
J. Jill
Jennifer's Garden
Joanna Gray of London
Jones & Jones
La Perfumerie
Le Four Francais
Leonard L. Greif, Jr.

Littlefields
Living Thin
Mano Swartz
Marson Galleries Ltd.
Maryland Craft & Antique Gallery
Mollett Travel. Inc.
Mondi
Nan Duskin
NationsBank
Nature's Cupboard of Love
Nettle Creek
Night Good
Noir
Octavia, Inc.
Party People

Pendelton
Pied Piper
Premier Vision
Radisson Hotel
Roland Park Florist
Roost Restaurant
Ruth Shaw, Inc.
Susan Kershaw Design
Sutton on the Run
Talbots
The Store Ltd.
Tobacco Merchant
Vibrant Knits
Village Flower Mart
Village Food Center
Williams-Sonoma

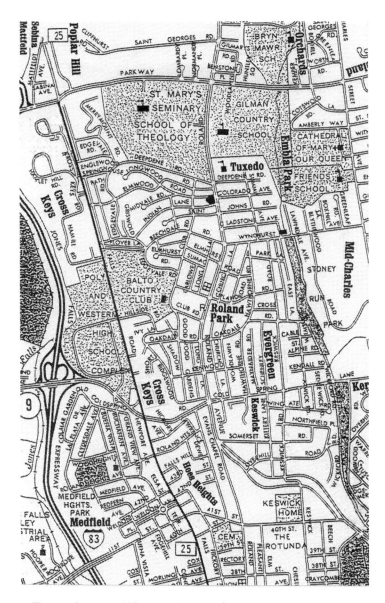

The two Cross Keys Villages and surrounding area. Map source: Karen Lewand, 1988.

Scott Settlement Historic District

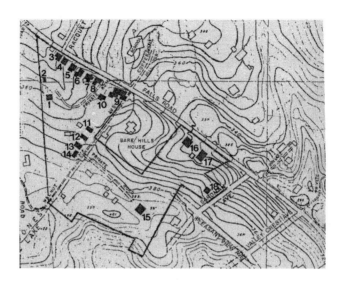

1 Aquilla Scott, Sr., rear of lot

2 Aquilla Scott, Jr., carriage house rear of lot

3 Matthew Yates, Sr., 6244 Falls Road

4 Matthew Yates, Jr., 6242

5 George A. Scott, 6240

6 Nathaniel Scott, 6238

7 Priscilla Scott, 6236

8 Ella Scott Moore, 6234

9 & 10 Store Building and Refreshment Stand, 6224-6228

11 Dorothy Glover, 1404 Walnut Avenue

12 John Barnes, 1406

13 Tyrone Smith, 1408

14 Eugene Warnock, 1410

15 Wright, 6230

16 William C. Jenkins, 6214-6216

17 John H. Dorsey, 6210-6212

18 Clarence E. Scott, 1404 Gardman Avenue

Bibliography

Books

Baldwin, Lewis V., "Schismatic Tendencies and Ecumenical Possibilities: The Struggles of Small African Methodist Bodies." *The AME Church Review,* Apr-June, 2001.

Branhall, Billie, *Reinventing Cities: Equity Planners Tell Their Stories,* Temple UP, 1994.

Brugger, Robert J., *Maryland: A Middle Temperament 1634–1980,* Baltimore: The Johns Hopkins UP, 1988.

Buckly, Julian A., "Picturesque County Buildings of Maryland," *The Architectural Review,* vol. 16, No.1, Jan 1901.

Clayton, Ralph, *Slavery, Slave Holdings of Antebellum Baltimore 1820–1870.* Bowie: Heritage 1993.

Coale, Joseph, M., III, *Middling Planters of Ruxton, 1694–1850.* Baltimore: Maryland Historical Society, 1996.

Cox, Joseph W. *Robert Goodloe Harper: The Evolution of a Southern Federalist Congressman.* Diss. Ann Arbor: Michigan U Microfilms, Inc., 1967.

Current Biography, Feb. 1982. vol. 43, no. 2

Dorsey, John and James D. Dilts, *A Guide to Baltimore Architecture, 3rd ed,* Centreville: Tidewater, 1997.

Farrell, Michael R. *The History of Baltimore's Streetcars.* Sykesville, Maryland 1992.

Fee, Elizabeth, Linda Shopes, and Linda Zeidman, eds. *The Baltimore Book: New Views of Local History.* Philadelphia: Temple UP, 1991.

Gibbons, Boyd, *Wye Island*, The Johns Hopkins UP, 1977.

Goodyear, Patricia, *Baltimore Country Club, One Hundred Years, 1898–1998,* self pub. 1998.

Hollifield, William, *Difficulties Made Easy: History of the Turnpikes of Baltimore City and County.* Baltimore County Historical Society, Cockeysville, Maryland. 1978.

Maryland Geologic Survey, vol. 3, Baltimore: The Johns Hopkins U P, 1899.

McCauley, Lois B., "Maryland Historical Prints 1752 to 1889" Baltimore: Maryland Historical Society, 1975.

McMillan, Joe, *Papal Heraldry, Arms of the Papacy,* http://flagspot.net/flags/va-swiss.html.

Miller, Mark, *Mt. Washington: Baltimore Suburb, A History revealed through Pictures and Narrative,* Baltimore: GBS, division of Gordon's Booksellers, 1980.

Morriss, Margaret Shove, *Colonial Trade of Maryland, 1689–1715,* The Johns Hopkins UP, Baltimore, Maryland, 1914.

Papenfuse, Eric Robert, *The Evils of Necessity: Robert Goodloe Harper and the Moral Dilemma of Slavery.* Philadelphia: American Philosophical Society, 1997.

Phillips, Kevin, *The Cousins' Wars,* New York: Basic Books, 1999.

Rouse, James W., *Autobiography,* unpub., Columbia, Maryland. n.d.

Ryon, Roderick N., *Northwest Baltimore and its Neighborhoods 1870–1970: Before Smart Growth,* U of Baltimore, 2000.

Sandler, Gilbert, "The Mount Washington Days of H. L. Mencken," *Menckeniana,* Quarterly Review of the Mencken Society, Summer, 1980.

Scott, Dolores B., *The Scotts of Falls Turnpike Road: A brief Family History,* unpub. 1983.

Tall, Luther S, *Memories of Growing up in Roland Park, 1902–1924,* self-pub, n.d.

Tobin, Jacqueline L., and Raymond G. Dobard, *Hidden in Plain View,* New York: Doubleday, 1999.

Weston, B. Latrobe, "Before Roland Park," *The Evening Sun,* 8 May 1934.

Periodicals

"Century of Memories: One hundred-year-old man living history for young-sters," *American Educator,* The Professional Journal of the American Federation of Teachers, vol. 3, no. 3, Fall 1979.

"Court finds defense leaky," *Engineering News Record,* 8 Jun 1989.

Jones, Malcolm Jr., "James Rouse Sparked New Life in Old Cities: A developer with a Sunday-school heart, New York: *Newsweek,* 22 Apr 1996.

"Roland Park Sewerage System" *Roland Park Review,* Nov 1910.

"Roland Park," *The Olmstedian,* vol. 13, issue 1, Fall 2001.

Semmes, Raphael, "Aboriginal Maryland 1608–1689," Baltimore: Maryland Historical Society, vol. XXIV, no. 3, Sep 1929.

"The Fall of the house of Harper," Roundtable, *Warfield's,* Apr 1989.

Weston, "Cross-Keys in the Line of Progress," *Roland Park Review,* May 1915.

Newspapers

Badham, Portia E., "Parker B. Douglass' memories of Baltimore." Baltimore: *Afro-American,* Baltimore, 7 July 1979.

Ettlin, David Michael, "Students tape centenarian's city memories." Baltimore: *The Sun,* 17 May 1979.

"How Roland Park was founded and Developed," Baltimore: *The Sun,* 27 Dec 1908.

Jones, Newbern, "Diploma for 100-year-old volunteer." Baltimore: *The News American*, 7 Jun 1979.

Olesker, Michael, "103 years of good memories" and "Centenarian's memory takes him back to McKinley, Great Fire." Baltimore: *The Evening Sun*, n.d.

Rasmussen, Frederick M, "Josephine Fenwick, valued independence: Octogenarian as storyteller," *The Sun*, 10 Mar 1995.

"Things you never knew before about Roland Park, *The Messenger*, Dec. 1976

Wilson, Kimberly A. C., "Woman, girl die in fire at house on Falls Road" Baltimore: *The Sun*, May 2002.

Vozzella, Laura, "Center inspires debate: Preservationists say Columbia site has historical value," Baltimore: *the Sun*, 24 Jun 2001.

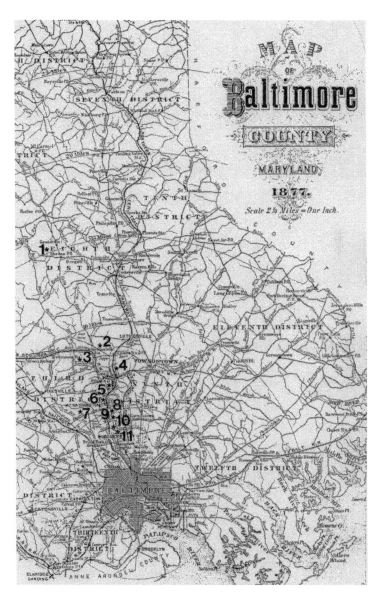

From top, **1** *Shawan, Cuba Rd., Oregon Ridge;* **2** *Brooklandville;* **3** *Rockland;* **4** *St. John's Chapel, parsonage and cemetery;* **5** *Lake Roland;* **6** *Bare Hills;* **7** *Mt. Washington;* **8** *Roland Park;* **9** *Village of Cross Keys and Cross Keys Village;* **10** *Coldspring La. and Falls Rd.;* **11** *Hampden Reservoir.*

Index

A

Addison, Joe "Josey" 51
African American ix, x, xi, xv, 1, 6, 7, 8, 9, 15, 27, 46, 54, 55, 59, 75, 85, 153, 154, 156
Allen, Richard 62
Allison, Nancy 101, 133
Altman, Rich 112, 114, 129, 130
American Colonization Society xv
American Revolution xi, 56
Askew, Monk x, 111, 128, 136, 137, 145, 148

B

Baker, Charles H. 80
Baker, Mrs. Charles 3
Baker, O. Parker 80
Baldwin, Lewis V. 62, 63
Baltimore ix, x, xi, xii, xiii, xiv, xv, xvi, xviii, xx, 1, 3, 4, 5, 6, 8, 19, 21, 22, 25, 27, 33, 34, 35, 39, 45, 47, 51, 54, 56, 57, 60, 61, 62, 64, 65, 67, 72, 74, 77, 78, 79, 80, 84, 85, 88, 91, 92, 93, 94, 95, 97, 98, 99, 100, 101, 102, 104, 105, 107, 108, 109, 110, 112, 113, 116, 117, 118, 120, 124, 125, 128, 130, 131, 132, 133, 134, 135, 136, 137, 139, 140, 142, 146, 149, 150, 151, 152, 153, 154, 167, 168, 169, 170
Baltimore & Susquehanna Railroad 5, 60, 61
Baltimore Country Club ix, xx, 21, 22, 34, 88, 97, 98, 99, 100, 104, 105, 117, 168
Baltimore Sun 3, 6, 8, 65, 84
Bare Hills ix, 1, 10, 27, 43, 45, 46, 47, 48, 49, 51, 53, 54, 55, 56, 57, 58, 59, 63, 66, 69, 72, 73, 80, 83, 86, 171
Bare Hills Historical District 55
Bart, Harry 91, 92, 93
Batchelor, Harry xix, 89
Baxter, Elizabeth xiii, xiv
Baxter, Wiley M. xiii
Bellona Avenue 61, 66, 67, 71, 72

Belluschi, Pietro 91, 109
Belmont, Augie xix, 92
Bouton, Edward H. 22, 120
Branhall, Billie 33
Brooklandville 171
Brooklets xv, xvi, xvii
Brown, Alexander 91
Brown, Ann 69
Brown, Charles 29
Brown, George N. 42, 81, 82, 83
Brown, Lola 69
Brown, Marie Scott x, 19, 45, 47, 48, 49, 50, 51, 52, 53, 54, 55, 56, 57, 58, 61, 67, 74
Brown, Sam 44, 52, 53
Brown, Thomas 59
Bruggman, Tom x, 4, 24

C

Calloway, Cab 22
Capron, Richard J. 1
Carroll, Catherine "Kitty" xi
Carroll, Reita Bryant 20, 27
Carter, Ann Gaskins 18
Caton, Richard 5
Chaney, Ed x, 27, 33, 42, 86
Charles Carroll of Carrollton ix, xi, xii, 5, 88
Charlottetown 92, 97
Cherry Hill 97, 99, 125
Chesapeake Habitat for Humanity 70
Clayton, Ralph x, 25, 57
Clemons, Shirley 15
Coates, Greg 57
Cochran, Alex 92
Cohen, Mark 137
Coker, Daniel 62
Coldspring Lane xii, 1, 3, 8, 18, 22, 37, 79, 80, 84, 85, 88, 131
Collins-Kronstadt and Associates 109

Columbia 106, 111, 112, 113, 114, 117, 119, 124, 126, 128, 129, 130, 135, 136, 137, 138, 145, 147, 150, 151
Community Research and Development 92, 104, 109
Connecticut General Life Insurance 106, 135
Cook, Susan 55
Cooke, Betty x, 88, 93, 115, 122, 124, 130
Cooke, Marie x, 55
CRD 92, 93, 94, 95, 99, 100, 102, 103, 104, 105, 106, 118, 124
Cross Keys Inn 1, 2, 5, 6, 13, 38, 40, 75, 79, 80, 83, 123, 124, 154, 161
Cross Keys Village ix, x, xi, xx, 1, 3, 4, 5, 6, 8, 9, 12, 15, 16, 17, 20, 24, 26, 27, 31, 32, 34, 36, 37, 40, 43, 44, 49, 53, 74, 75, 76, 77, 78, 79, 80, 81, 83, 84, 85, 86, 87, 90, 98, 99, 104, 111, 114, 153, 154, 156, 160, 163, 171
CVS Pharmacy 1, 25, 38, 40, 81

D

Daniels, Ned ix, 90, 93, 96, 101, 102, 114, 118, 120, 122, 123, 125, 128, 129, 130, 133
Davis, Amy x, 54
DeFilippo, Frank x, 132
Derricks, Louise 46
DeVito, Mathias J. 126
DeVito, Matt 126, 127, 130, 134, 138, 139, 140, 141, 142, 143, 144, 145, 147, 148
Disney, Walt 96
Ditch, Scott x, 110, 111, 113, 115, 117, 118, 135, 136
Douglass, Frederick 34, 76
Douglass, Michael 33
Douglass, Parker 76, 77
Dowling, Robert 91
Dugan, Octavia 120
Durham, Walter 114

E

Eastern Shore xvi, 56, 57, 58, 62, 102, 135
Easton, Md. xv, xvii
Engineering News Record 147, 169
Enterprise Development Corporation 142, 143
Enterprise Foundation 102, 126, 141, 143

F

Falls Road ix, xi, xiii, xx, 1, 3, 4, 5, 6, 7, 8, 11, 12, 15, 16, 17, 18, 20, 21, 22, 23, 24, 26, 27, 28, 29, 30, 31, 32, 33, 34, 35, 36, 37, 39, 40, 41, 42, 43, 44, 45, 46, 49, 51, 53, 55, 56, 63, 64, 67, 69, 73, 75, 76, 77, 78, 79, 80, 81, 83, 84, 85, 86, 98, 99, 100, 104, 105, 106, 107, 109, 123, 131, 133, 153, 156, 157, 170
Falls Road AME 6, 7, 27, 31, 37, 53, 78, 83, 156
Falls Turnpike Road 4, 58, 168
Faneuil Hall 137, 138, 139
Finley, Bill 112, 113, 130
Fishpaw, Elijah 60
Frey, Gladys-Marie 24
Fugitive Slave Law 59

G

Gambrill, John 6
Gambrill, Nelson 6
Gardman, John 48, 69
Gatehouse 106, 117, 118, 119, 124, 133, 160
Gehry, Frank O. 111, 119, 128, 134, 145, 147
Gibson Island 22, 99
Gillett, Jack x, 132
Gough, Anar 64
Great Baltimore Fire 77
Griswold, III, Alexander Brown 91
Gruen, Victor 93, 94, 99

H

Hall, Joyce 96
Hall, Margaret 168
Hall, Vertelle x, 36, 43, 76, 82, 83
Hammond, Caroline 78, 79
Harborplace 136, 137, 140, 142, 143
Harlem Movie Theater 82
Harper House 113, 128, 129, 135, 138, 145, 146, 147, 150, 152, 159
Harper, Robert Goodloe ix, xi, xii, xiv, xv, xvi, 8, 60, 88, 120, 135, 153, 167, 168
Harundale 93, 94, 95, 103
Harvard University 96
Harwood, Herb x
Hawkins, Eliza 61, 62

Hawkins, Jesse x, 27, 29, 82, 84
Hawks, John 53
Hawks, Rachel 53
Hector's Hopyard 60, 63, 72
Hillside Road 1, 8, 17, 18, 82, 85
Hinze, Fred x, xiii, xiv
Hoe, Aunt Lucy 7
Hoes Heights 7, 27, 40, 52
Hoes, Jr., Charles Grandison 7
Hollifield, William x, 2, 80
Hollins Station 45, 46, 48
Hollyday, Guy T. O. xviii, 120
Hook, Johnza 63
Hoppenfeld, Mort 102, 112, 113, 114, 128
Huddles, Gary 124
Hynson, Jerry x, 24, 27, 31, 33, 75, 76, 78

J

James W. Rouse & Company 91, 95, 102,
    106, 118, 120, 124
Jenkins, Charles "Chilli" 89
Jim Crow 19
Johns Hopkins Hospital xvi, 75, 93, 150
Johnson, Delores 27, 41
Johnson, Paul M. x, 3, 36, 37, 38, 39, 40, 158
Jones Falls ix, xi, xii, xx, 3, 4, 5, 12, 21, 22,
    23, 24, 28, 37, 39, 45, 63, 85, 88, 97, 99,
    104, 106, 107, 112, 113, 124, 128, 131,
    134
Jones Falls Expressway 85, 97, 107, 112, 124
Jones, David 4

K

Kelly, W. Boulton "Bo" 90, 95
Kilberg, Al x, 145
Knight, Perry 6, 79, 80, 84
Kornblatt, David W. 128
Kutch, Sally x, 29

L

Latrobe, Benjamin H. xiii, xiv, xviii, xix, xx
Lee, Tony x, 23, 33
LeVere, Carolyn Scott x, 56, 72, 73, 74
Liberia xv
Loomis, Lee xix, 92
Lord, Sarah Fenno 55, 59
Luetkemeyer, John 121, 122

M

ManorCare 26, 37, 38, 39, 76
Marshall, Thurgood 22, 149
Mason, Ben x, 41
McBride, Charley 23
McBride, John x, 23, 27, 81, 82
McBride, Sharon x, 21, 26, 27
McClane, Hector 63
McDonald, William "Billie" 79
Memorial Stadium 123
Mencken, H. L. 107, 108, 168
Metropolitan Research and Development xix
Meyerhoff, Jack 92, 93, 102
Miss Bettie's Café 38
Mondawmin xx, 91, 92, 101, 116, 130
Moss, Hunter xviii, xix, xx, 88, 91
Moss-Rouse Company xviii, xix, 89, 91
Mowbray, Col. John McC. 103
Mt. Washington 1, 13, 22, 41, 46, 47, 53,
    63, 64, 74, 83, 113, 131, 168
Murray and Fleiss 120

N

Nash, Ogden 148, 149
National Register of Historic Places 69
Native Americans 4
Neel, Sam xix, 92
Northern Central Railway 5, 71
Northern Parkway xii, xx, 20, 42, 107, 108

O

O'Donovan, Gail ix, 66, 67, 69
Oakdale Road xiv, 22, 37, 38, 39, 44, 156
Oakland xi, xii, xiii, xiv, xv, xvi, 8, 37, 88
Olmsted, Jr., Frederick Law 109
Osborne, Margie 131

P

Palmer, Ernestine x, 40
Parker, Anthony "Tony" 15
Parker, Arthur Grafton 15
Parker, Bartholomew 15
Parker, Holly 15, 16, 17, 27, 31, 57, 75
Parker, Tony 15, 16, 17, 27, 31, 57, 75
Pascault, C. O'Donnell 114
Pascault, Lydia "Dia" 92

Pennington, Emily Harper xv, xvi
Perky, Henry 112
Phillips, Priscilla Scott 74
Ponselle, Rosa 51
Poole, Robert 76, 77

Q

Quarters 114 xix

R

Randall, June 18
Republic of Oread 112
Ridgewood Road 3, 8, 9, 11, 30, 34, 80
Rockland Mills 4, 5
Roland Green 150, 159
Roland Park ix, xi, xii, xiii, xiv, xvi, xx, 1, 3, 4, 7, 8, 9, 10, 11, 12, 13, 14, 15, 17, 18, 22, 32, 33, 34, 35, 36, 39, 50, 51, 53, 75, 79, 82, 84, 88, 97, 98, 100, 103, 104, 105, 106, 107, 109, 111, 113, 117, 119, 120, 129, 130, 135, 153, 154, 162, 168, 169, 170, 171
Roland Park Civic League 8, 100, 129
Roland Park Review 8, 12, 169
Roost Restaurant 120, 162
Rouse, James W. 91, 95, 100, 102, 106, 118, 120, 124, 141
Rouse, Jim xv, xvi, xvii, xviii, xvix, xx, 89, 90, 91, 92, 93, 94, 95, 96, 97, 99, 100, 101, 102, 103, 149, 150, 151, 152, 153, 154
Rouse, Libby xviii, 95, 114, 115, 133
Rouse, Patty 137
Rouse, Willard "Bill" xvii, xx, 89, 91, 102, 130
Rouse, Willard, Jr. xvi, xvii
Rumford, Trixie 121
Ruxton ix, 26, 35, 48, 49, 53, 54, 60, 61, 62, 63, 64, 67, 71, 72, 74, 99, 117, 167

S

Sally Jones 121
Sandler, Gilbert x, 107
Santa Monica Place 135, 145
Schaefer, Mayor William Donald 139, 140
Scott, Delores B. 61
Scott, III, William Walter 61
Scott, Jr., James Aquilla 63
Scott, Jr., Simon 80

Scott, M.D., Douglas Grant 75
Scott, Rev. Edward W. 15, 26, 65, 66, 74, 75
Scott, Sr., James Aquilla 58
Seabreeze, Charles x, 17, 27
Shannahan, Polly x, 93
Silva, Delores x, 23, 27, 83
Slave ix, xiii, xiv, xv, 16, 24, 25, 56, 57, 59, 60, 62, 64, 77, 78, 133, 167
Somerville, Frank P. L. 85
Spath, Anton 13, 104
Spath Tract 103, 104, 105, 106, 124
Spear, Mike 136, 147
Spies, Tom x, 67, 68, 70
Spring Gardens 5
St. John's Chapel ix, 50, 54, 64, 65, 66, 67, 68, 71, 72, 171
St. Mary's County 56, 57, 58
St. Paul Garage xviii, 110
Stauffer, Richard C. 109
Steinmetz, Bill x, 88, 90, 122
Stillson, George 89, 102
STP 57
Struever, C. William 151
Symington, Thomas S. 34

T

Talbottown 92, 93, 94
Taylor, Peter 4
Temmink, Bill x, 35
The Store Ltd. 90, 121, 125, 162
The Village of Cross Keys ix, x, xi, xii, xx, 3, 12, 88, 90, 97, 99, 103, 106, 107, 108, 109, 112, 113, 124, 128, 129, 131, 132, 134, 135, 137, 138, 142, 147, 150, 152, 154, 159, 171
Thompson, Benjamin 136
Time magazine 142
Tipper, Charlie x, 67, 68, 69
Title Guarantee and Trust Company xviii
Tobacco 5, 56, 63, 162
Tobias ix, 16, 45, 56, 57, 153
Tollgate 5, 77, 79
Tom Thumb Wedding 33, 41
Towers, Adm. Jack xix
Tripp, David x
Tyson AUMP Church 26, 74, 157
Tyson, Elisha 26

U

Underground railroad 24, 59, 78
Union 26, 34, 61, 62, 63, 113
Urban Renewal 33, 85, 86, 93, 142

V

Village Food Center 149, 162
Village Management 150, 160
Village Square 90, 99, 106, 109, 114, 115, 118, 120, 121, 122, 123, 125, 129, 130, 136, 149, 154, 160

W

Walsh, Ann ix, 35
Waring, Col. George E. 22
Waverly Tower 93

Wesorts 57
West, Gertrude 29
Weston, B. Latrobe 8
White Oak Grove 3, 6, 13, 28, 40, 80, 81, 156
White, "Doc" 41
White, Mayor Kevin 138
Wilde, Frazar 135
Williams, Eugene 32
Willse, Sally G. 72
Wollon, Jim 70
Woodberry 5, 26, 77, 79, 113, 133
Woods, Hiram 113
Wye Island 135, 136, 168

Y

Yates, Mathew 55

0-595-27358-0

Made in the USA
Middletown, DE
28 June 2020